PRAISE FOR *RESPOND UP*

"This book will be a life message for countless ⁀ople. Don does an incredible job challenging us to live ᵗ first life despite what the world throws our way. I h꜀ ᵗ on-ally inspired to prepare to respond inste ᴀs things come."

—Justin Dailey, Lead P ᴊhurch ᴊ, Florida

"Life is filled with twists and turns, ar. ɾhrow some very unexpected and unwelcome tɾ. ⁄ay! What we do then determines whether we grow b꜀. or whether we grow better. Penetrating and probing, *Respond Up* will help you find and unlock God's best for your future! I heartily rec-ommend it!"

—Ron Johnson, Pastor of One Church
in Orlando, Florida

"React OR respond! Brilliant!! Don Newman has broken free of the status quo for our attitude toward life's events and the leadership it models. Weaving personal stories, like only he can, with timeless biblical observation against the back-drop of the classic scriptural account of the life of Joseph, Don takes the reader on a journey of laughter, tears, and self-accountability. By being so transparent with his own suc-cesses and failures, Don gently holds them up for the reader as a mirror into the heart. *Respond Up* is a must-read and must-keep for any library. I highly, highly (did I say highly?) recommend this well-written book to all those who desire to MOVE UP!"

—Kevin Craig, Lead Pastor, Thrive Church
in Apopka, Florida

"I first met Don when he visited Wales several years ago, and met a man whose heart was full of God. We spent some time together and he ministered powerfully, but what really impressed me was the man in private. He spoke spiritual wisdom into my family and me. This book is not just another book on 'getting better at being you.' It's a book written by a man who doesn't just have head knowledge about life, but by a man with a heart full of life and love as a result of 'responding up.'

A good person produces good things from the treasury of a good heart, and an evil person produces evil things from the treasury of an evil heart. What you say flows from what is in your heart (Luke 6:45)."

—Bill Chapman, Senior Leader,
Myrtle House, Llanelli, South Wales

"Responding to the calling of God to shepherd people has got to be the most difficult task on earth. Above all other attributes that this calling mandates, the ability to be let down or downright assaulted by the very people you give your life to serve will tend to rip the heart right out of most men. Don Newman has walked miles as a shepherd and has undoubtedly known the highs as well as the lows associated with his calling. He could only be writing his new book *Respond Up* from the perspective of a leader who has had to learn the only way to win is up! God and you make the majority. Once you've burned the boats and really learned to rely only on the help that comes from above, will you then begin to fly on the wings God created for you! Good job, Don. Thanks for reminding us all where to look!"

—Pastor G.F. Watkins,
Gfwatkinsministries.com, Katy, Texas

"I love Don's transparency as he writes. I am certain you will find it refreshing. It's not a surprise. Having known him and Tracee for more than a decade, this is the trait that made them such effective leaders. They are approachable, relatable, and more importantly their seasoned wisdom has been beneficial. Today Don has been graced to help leaders around the nation rise above their own limitations and achieve their God given potential. Now, through *Respond Up*, Don is offering you a helping hand to take that next big step. Don't pass it up!"

—Daniel Norris, Author,
Evangelist, Producer,
Trailoffire.org

"Life is full of challenges and obstacles. My good friend Don has taken Joseph's story from the Bible and leveraged it with his past experiences as a state trooper, football coach, and pastor to create a life manual full of valuable insights. A biblically-consistent approach that encourages and guides readers to face rejection, delay, disappointment, and opposition head on and always respond up."

—Ted Jones, Entrepreneur,
Former High School Basketball Coach,
and Author of *Springing Forward*

"Wow! If I had Donald Newman's book *Respond Up* years ago it would have saved me precious time and resources. I agree with Donald that God's kingdom is filled with leaders. This book shows us how to respond to the call of leadership in our lives. I highly recommend this book for anyone ready to respond to the call of God in their life."

—Dr. Robert Watkins, Senior Leader
of Conquer Worldwide

"Don eloquently uses the 'dance card' analogy to describe the importance of making the correct decisions as to how we fill out our dance card as we proceed through life. The book provides an excellent road map for all of us as we traverse the many challenges faced here on earth. The importance of God, and how He can be such a positive influence on our decision making process, is discussed throughout each chapter of the book.

"The book provides insight as to how each of us are actually leaders in our own sphere of influence. It just depends on how we choose to use the leadership qualities God has given us. At some point, all of us must take on the role of a leader, whether it is making decisions at work, for an organization we belong to, or in resolving a family matter requiring the ability to make good sound judgments. We all have leadership qualities; the important question is how we make use of those qualities.

"As the book describes, we can all be leaders when called on to do so. What we must all remember is we must rise to the challenges we face, and respond up to those challenges, not merely react to them.

"Don, congratulations on a very well-written and informative book that should be a must-read for all aspiring leaders, and all of us who are required to make decisions during the course of our lives."

—Ron Grimming, Director Florida
Highway Patrol (Retired)

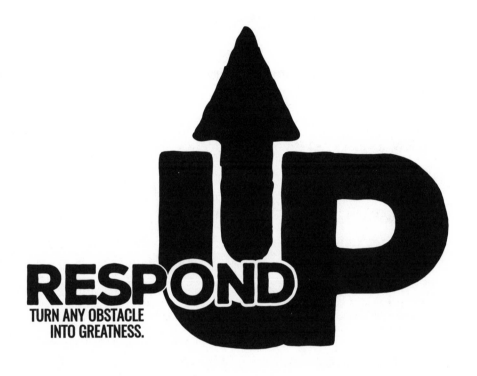

RESPOND UP
TURN ANY OBSTACLE
INTO GREATNESS.

Don Newman

www.coachdonnewman.com

2301 Lucien Way #415
Maitland, FL 32751
407.339.4217
www.302books.com

TABLE OF CONTENTS

FOREWORD

Respond UP! Don't react down!

I met Don Newman almost two decades ago when I was co-pastoring a church plant in Orlando. He and Tracee became leaders in our congregation. Later, Don joined our church staff and grew in ministry over the years, serving as a pastor, marketplace Christian business leader, publisher, coach, and author.

A dynamic teacher, speaker, and motivator, Don walks out in real life what he talks and teaches. I had the privilege of giving input on *Respond Up*. Our dialogue on this dynamic, life-changing book powerfully impacted my attitudes and responses in all my relationships. This book will not only inform you; you will be inspired and impacted through the practical insights Don shares in these pages.

Here's some of what you will discover:

- The way you move forward *in* life is greatly dictated by how you respond *to* life.
- Life happens, and we can either "react" or learn to "respond."

- Choosing to respond instead of reacting out of our past patterns not only leads us forward, but can also be the key to promotion.
- There is a big difference between choosing to become a "first-responder" and just being a "first-reactor."
- The real power to become a person who responds instead of reacts comes from where your response begins...respond up!

Don's message presents the life of Joseph as a pattern for you and I to follow. When you look at how Joseph responded to rejection, betrayal, temptation, power and authority, you'll learn how to respond positively to others. Through his story, you'll discover that life sets up the greatest opportunities for advancement in the everyday challenges and opportunities.

Respond Up is all about your choice to answer life by responding to God first. When "life happens" to you, you could react and get angry, you could try to fix it yourself, you could do nothing at all, or you can respond up by turning to God.

I hope I have given you enough salty tidbits in this brief overview to make you hungry and thirsty for devouring this whole book now! Get out your notepad, journal, or tablet. You will jot down self-talk declarations and tips that will change your responses, conversations, retorts, and attitudes as you "respond up!"

-Dr. Larry Keefauver,
Best-Selling Author
and International Teacher

INTRODUCTION

It's undeniable: the world we live in today is hand-shaped by those whom we call "leaders." In fact, these leaders carry a special responsibility for shaping the upcoming generation who will one day replace them. No one would disagree that developing great leaders is an important task (thus the focus of this book), because as John Maxwell said, "Everything rises or falls upon leadership."[1] God calls each of us to some form of influence; He loves using His people to impact the earth. His kingdom here is teeming with holy pacesetters! Some just don't know they are called yet, while others don't know how to get there.

This book is all about the specific ways God selects and develops His righteous ringleaders. Within each of us waits a leader, ready to be raised up and called to action. To get there, it's vital to understand what instigates our transformation into an extraordinary influencer. If our hope is to continue to see great leaders emerge, it's time to quit looking to how *man* makes leaders and explore how *God* does it. What kind of crazy circumstances does God use to call and qualify those He chooses? How does He decide who is next in His batting order? What is God looking for when He reaches down His mighty hand and pulls someone from the unknown to prominence and position? Think about it: how did He take a lowly shepherd boy named David all the way from the pasture to the palace—and what did David do that opened that door?

Have you ever thought about where real leadership comes from? How does it even begin? The Bible contains many stories of people who succeeded or failed in their quest to have influence. Can anyone enlist, or is there more to it? Psalm 75:6-7 says, "For promotion and power come from nowhere on earth, but only from God. He promotes one and deposes another" (TLB). Ultimately, what is the difference between those God promotes and those He doesn't?

If God is the one who hands down the mantle of real leadership—the eternal kind that changes lives and destinies for good—then how does He give it? Is there a secret we can learn and cooperate with?

ARE LEADERS BORN OR TAUGHT?

Leaders come in different shapes and sizes, and from different backgrounds, too. There have been notoriously short leaders, such as Napoleon, and tall leaders, such as King Henry VIII (who stood at 6'4"), and William Wallace, the man played brilliantly by Mel Gibson in the movie *Braveheart*, who was 6'7". Many legendary women shaped our world as well: Rosa Parks, Joan of Arc, and Queen Victoria, who ushered us into the Victorian Era, a time of great medical, scientific, and technological advancement.

You don't have to be tall, short, fat, skinny, male, or female in order to be an effective leader. You also do not have to come from a family of wealth or influence. What you need to understand, unequivocally, is that God called you to be a forerunner. Which brings us to the greatest question of this book: will you answer the call and be another agent of change in this time?

There are two trains of thought: leaders are either born, or leaders are taught. Both statements are true. However, it's only those who master the keys to *learning* leadership that reach the pinnacle they're destined to reach. For those who are taught, there is a hidden bedrock of knowledge which allowed them to expand beyond their original sphere of influence. This foundation can only be built when there is a willingness to be taught.

> The foundation of truly great leaders is built on this truth: it's not how we choose to act, but rather how we choose to respond, which eventually fits us for leadership.

The foundation of truly great leaders is built on this truth: it's not how we choose to act, but rather how we choose to respond, which eventually fits us for leadership. The decision to respond correctly to what life throws at us may be the most important decision any potential leader can make. Notice, I said respond and not react; there is a marked difference between being a "reactor" and a "responder," which we'll cover later in this book.

Most of the steps taken up the ladder of success are steps of responding correctly, or what I call "responding up."

Think about it: every decision we make has an outward impact on the world we live in. First, it changes us, and through that change we receive deeper measures of influence. Why do our choices provide greater opportunities? I believe it's the plan of God. As we are changed, so is our ability to lead. In short, the level of our influence is inextricably linked to our level of character.

Leadership is not as much about a title as it is about having influence upon others. In the end, good leadership is never about position, but results—results that create positive impact and transformation for others. Think about the greatest leaders you know, both publically and personally. Did their mentorship change you for the better? How did they influence you or others?

> Everyday life is made up of more than just mere occurrences; it's packed with well-hidden opportunities to grow you into the leader you were meant to be.

The point of leadership is to serve the good of others, but the initial impact must begin within the leader. The real key to developing others is discovered while developing yourself first. That's God's ultimate plan: that the change He brings in you will become the influence you have on others. Everyday life is made up of more than just mere occurrences; it's packed with well-hidden opportunities to grow you into the leader you were meant to be.

Has anyone told you that you're the catalyst for change in your family, your friends, your workplace, and in your community? Do you know you were not created to fade into the background of life? Our God, who knew you before you were born, has destined for you to do great things with your time here on earth. Sadly, many believers never understand that. They go through their entire lives as wallflowers, like extras on a movie set. They profess to serve God; yet their lives are lived without ever stirring up so much as a ripple in the river of life. They have seeds of leadership deep within them, but never experience the full harvest. I believe God has a better plan for us than many of us have for ourselves—and in this book, we'll explore how to unlock that plan.

REAL LEADERSHIP

Real leadership is grounded in our calling to become a servant of Christ. When Jesus was asked in Matthew 22:37-39 what the most important commandment was, He answered, "Love the Lord your God with all your heart and with all your soul and with all your mind. This is the first and greatest commandment. And the second is like it: Love your neighbor as yourself" (NIV). That is what real leadership is all about!

Notice, the disciples didn't ask Him about the *two* most important commandments; they only asked about the most important. However, Jesus felt it was crucial to command us that we also need to love one another. We need to be of service to one another, to help one another, to provide support for one another. Those are acts of leadership. You are called to be a leader. Period. Now, welcome to the wonderful world of servant-leadership.

So where can we find God's plan for becoming the stalwart of influence we're destined to be? Are there patterns in God's word to reveal how God develops great mentors? Are there any great authorities who've left us a roadmap to follow?

LEARN FROM JOSEPH

This book follows the life of Joseph. As you read about his journey, scripted out for us in the book of Genesis, you will see a pattern emerge: one that demonstrates how we can press on in the most difficult challenges and end up in a great place of leadership. Buried in his story is God's plan for creating leaders who make a real difference. My story follows the same pattern; I've learned that my next promotion *in* life is always based on my last response *to* life. *Respond Up* is filled with discoveries and discernments from my own journey, and that of Joseph. When we see how Joseph clung to a specific perspective as he was hit with trial after trial, it's clear there is a pattern to moving from the pit to the palace: every trial in his life was also a catalyst. Joseph's unimaginable hardships were preparation for him to become one of the greatest leaders found in God's holy word.

"Now Jacob dwelt in the land where his father was a stranger, in the land of Canaan. This is the history of Jacob.

Joseph, being seventeen years old, was feeding the flock with his brothers. And the lad was with the sons of Bilhah and the sons of Zilpah, his father's wives; and Joseph brought a bad report of them to his father.

Now Israel loved Joseph more than all his children, because he was the son of his old age. Also he made him a tunic of many colors. But when his brothers saw that their father loved him more than all his brothers, they hated him and could not speak peaceably to him."

Gen. 37:1-4

CHAPTER 1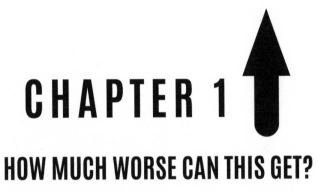

HOW MUCH WORSE CAN THIS GET?

There I was, sitting in the driver's seat of my car–if you could call what was left of it a car—asking myself if things could possibly get any worse. I had just been horribly rear-ended with my car tossed into a ditch. It was one of those things you hear about happening to others, but never plan for it to happen to *you*. The shock of the accident had me reeling and shaking, but as hard as that moment was, it was there in a random ditch off Glade Road where I heard the voice of God.

He told me one of the most crucial things I'd ever hear; the whole basis for this book. It is important to listen for God's voice in the quiet of the day—but it's absolutely vital to listen for His voice in the chaos of the storm.

> It is important to listen for God's voice in the quiet of the day–but it's absolutely vital to listen for His voice in the chaos of the storm.

Trust me, when your car is totaled and you're covered in glass, metal, and everything else you can imagine, you are suddenly open to hearing God. In fact, you have nothing else to do but listen. This was my time to hear Him, and what followed was a decision that would change the trajectory of my life forever.

A few weeks before the accident, I had arrived at a place of transition in my life—I had made a step of faith as instructed by God, but the outcome was very unlike what I imagined. Add a car accident to the mix, and I suddenly needed my faith more than ever. It was in this uncomfortable setting, this place of much-needed faith, that I realized I required a whole lot more "PGD"—Pure God Dependence—if I was going to make it through.

It was just eighteen months earlier when the possibility of moving to Texas to work with my former youth pastor and spiritual hero presented itself. The idea was first discussed on a ministry trip in London a year earlier. I still remember the excitement I felt as I contemplated the possibility of joining him. Aren't you thankful for the way your heart and imagination can be seized by a dream? I am—back then and still today—a dreamer at my core.

The dream became a reality: on December 31, 2003, my wife Tracee, my son Hunter, and I left Orlando, Florida and headed to Dallas, Texas. We'd be joining the staff of his newly-planted church, just as I'd envisioned. We were like Abraham;

> **Aren't you thankful for the way your heart and imagination can be seized by a dream?**

leaving the familiar to follow God into uncharted territory. Our family left Florida with one car, one big moving truck full of belongings, and the dream of an exciting future. The entire world was celebrating a brand new year, and I was celebrating a brand new chapter—but there was no way I could have anticipated the test waiting just around the corner.

As I adjusted to my new position on his staff, everything was a dream. Being a pastor with a strong gifting for developing leaders, I was given the task of launching the new home groups. Week after week went by; it seemed I was gifted for the role and God was blessing me in it. In a short time, we had developed many great servants of God and a process for sustaining future growth. I had followed God, and the dream was unfolding exactly as I'd hoped it would. But my comfortable dream was about to transform into a boot camp of spiritual testing.

A year and a half in, it was becoming clearer by the day that God was changing the playbook in my life. He was about to call a play I was not prepared for or expecting. The audible that God called brought me to a personal crossroads.

Have you ever embarked on a life journey only to realize later you weren't headed to a destination, but a bridge? This bridge led you somewhere entirely different than the endpoint you originally hoped for. Nothing is wrong with bridges—as long as they lead somewhere better, right? At those moments, questions beckon:

- How does one learn to trust God when everything appears untrustworthy?
- Who do you become when you stand in the face of adversity?
- How do we learn how to respond correctly, when reaction is an impulse driven from the core of our being?

Just before my accident, I had realized that my position with the church was not going to continue. This change arrived unexpectedly, but God used it to slowly grow the desire inside me to plant a church myself.

At first I thought church-planting was something I'd undertake in five or ten years; after all, I had only been at the church in Texas for eighteen months. Anyone who knows me well will tell you: until then, I never carried a desire to plant a church or even the desire to be the senior pastor of an established one. I knew the pressures those leaders went through, and I found the ride much more enjoy-able from the second, third, or even fourth seat. For a year and a half, I

However, as He often does, God was about to interrupt my comfort zone.

enjoyed being a pivotal leader within a growing congregation. I loved the pastor, the people, and the potential of what was to come. It wasn't on my bucket list to plant a church, but apparently it was on God's. However, as He often does, God was about to interrupt my comfort zone.

I would love to say we pulled off a perfect transition, leaving that church staff I loved. I do know that in the end we really tried to honor everyone, even amidst saying yes to what God called us to do. However, it's sometimes difficult to please God and please man at the same time. As leaders follow God, it can sometimes even feel like you're making a mistake. If our top goal is to never make a mistake in the journey,

Fear of making mistakes leads to the greatest mistake of all: never trying.

then there will most likely never be a journey to make a mistake on. Fear of making mistakes leads to the greatest mistake of all: never trying.

Because we didn't want to interfere with the church we were leaving, we made the decision to go back to Florida instead of staying in Texas. Our family and support systems were in Florida, as well as the pastor and church I served with before moving to Texas, and many of our friends. Being back in Florida meant we could launch with the best chance of success. Here we were, going back to Florida without jobs or even a place to live. In fact, we had just bought a house in Texas and now we'd have to sell it.

There were people throughout this experience who quietly said maybe I missed God; that I was never supposed to go to Texas anyway and should have stayed in Florida. I can't blame them for thinking that—I actually thought it myself once or twice—but there were two things I knew. I knew God called us to go, and I knew God would use that journey to change my life forever. Sadly, sometimes we think if something doesn't work

> We pin blame here, drop blame there, when all God wants is for us to fix our eyes on Him.

out exactly as we plan, God was never in it, and He never directed us to do it. I believe God is more interested in who we eventually become than in our immediate success. He will steer us straight into disappointment to make us greater than we could've ever become without it.

It's a wonderful mystery how God takes fallen man, in a fallen world, and fashions him into the beautiful image of His Son. We may look up to discover we're on a journey we didn't buy a map for, but whether or not we reach the destination is determined by how we choose to respond. When disaster strikes, most of us revert to "Blame Distribution." We pin blame here, drop blame there, when all God wants is for us to fix our eyes on Him. When we follow God's GPS, we can be led where He wants us to go.

THE MOST IMPORTANT THING I'VE EVER HEARD

So there I was on Glade Road, after paying one last visit to the church office to say goodbye. In another week, my son would finish his school year and we would drive to Florida. We had a lot on our plate: finding a house in Florida, selling our house in Texas, getting jobs, and of course, finding the location where God wanted us to plant His new church. My wife Tracee had already gone back the week before to find a place for us to live. Our daughters, Brittnee and Ashlee, were attending college in Florida and awaiting our return.

I can still remember the crash: I had just left the church office and was on my way home when traffic stopped. While I slowed and stopped safely behind the car in front of me, a work truck pulling a landscape trailer did not stop safely behind me. The driver of the truck had been checking his phone and plowed into the back of my car, ramming my vehicle into the one in front of me. For a moment I was smashed between these two vehicles, then somehow the force of the crash spun me into the ditch. I wasn't badly injured, but my car was totaled. I just sat there, thinking to myself, "Could the timing of this accident be any worse?" Here I was with no job, no place to live, and now I no longer had a car to drive back to Florida. Had God really called me to step out, or was this accident punishment for disobeying Him?

It was then and there, in the eye of the storm, when I heard the words I'll never forget. Words from a place deep within me, a place where God speaks and my spirit truly hears. Those words felt like balm to my soul. That was the beginning of my new journey. As I sat in my car, covered in glass and dirt, there was a moment of silence, a pause that transfixed me. It's then I heard God speak softly and clearly deep within my heart. "Choose your attitude wisely Don, because you will remember it for the rest of your life."

> **"Choose your attitude wisely Don, because you will remember it for the rest of your life."**

CHOOSE JOY!

I felt a strange peace as I looked around at my car and the cars of everyone else. I knew instinctively that what God said to me could only mean one thing: He was asking me to respond with an attitude of faith. God was asking me to choose joy! I can't tell you how I knew that; I just knew in the middle of this grim situation I had an opportunity to choose to trust God. Deep inside I understood all of this would eventually work out for my good.

> **"My brethren, count it all joy when you fall into various trials." James 1:2**

Now, when life is at its hardest, I like to say we should count it all as joy: "My brethren, count it all joy when you fall into various trials" (James 1:2).

Believe me: there was not one ounce of joy in me when I was sitting in my wrecked car in that ditch. Instead, there was a nagging feeling, attempting to confirm I'd really blown it this time; that I had made a huge mistake. We always seem to think this way when tragedy or difficult times arrive in our lives. We are convinced we've either done wrong or deserve what is happening to us. When you combine self-doubt ("did you really hear God on this one, or are you doing this all on your own?") with the pain of disappointment, you can really begin to spiral down the long and lonely descent of despair. You must find a way to choose joy!

That afternoon in May, I made a choice based on knowing God's voice and His word. I chose to *respond* instead of *react*.

REACTING VS. RESPONDING

Is there a difference between responding and reacting? Most of us use those words interchangeably, but they denote two totally different motivations, two different directions chosen when faced with a decision.

To "react" is to act on your first impulse. It's usually motivated by emotion, and often without much thought or reflection. There are circumstances in which we must react quickly, and an off-the-cuff answer is in order. Reactions are second nature to us; they come from our heart or from our soul. Sometimes, however, our reactions are wrong and can create destructive ripples as they bounce off of our fallen nature. To "respond" is to act with some other input outside of our emotion alone.

> To "respond" is to act with some other input outside of our emotion alone.

The word respond implies that thought, reason, wisdom, or even experience is added to our answer. I like to think that a response is just a reaction with a pause; a pause to think, reflect, and choose the best reaction possible. Then there are times we need to do more than pause and think; we need to pause and *hear*, hear what God is saying.

This is what I call *responding up*. It's the choice to turn to God, before I turn to give my reaction. It's what I did that day on Glade Road as I sat in my totaled car—and it changed my life forever.

In that moment, as I responded up, I knew He was with me and I was with Him. I did not make my choice based upon my feelings. The choice would've been different if I had done so. Instead, I stepped out of my dam-aged car in faith and walked out my response one step after the other. I took in the fresh air, shook the glass from my shirt, and went to check on the welfare of the other drivers. I responded up by choosing joy over anger or despair.

> **Don't make an internal decision without taking an outward action.**

Anytime you choose a course of action opposite to your own emotions and will, it is important to take a physical step of action that makes it real. If you make a commitment to for-give a family member, a friend, or even a co-worker, *you* must make the trip, *you* must write the letter, *you* must make the call. Don't make an internal decision without taking an outward action. Taking some type of action is absolutely crucial. Maybe that action is confessing something in the presence of a trusted friend. Other times it's deciding to stop going to certain places, and other times it's a deliberate decision to spend your time and resources differently. You can make an internal decision first, but it must be followed by an outward step. That step puts your obedience in motion and helps you end up with a lasting result instead of a momentary emotion that just feels like obedience. You need to understand: obedience costs something. Better yet, real obedience, at times, will cost everything.

My decision to get out of my car and help others—including the man who totaled my almost-completely-paid-off car—was not just a formal agreement in obedience, but a down payment toward following through with what God told me to do.

> God's way of choosing and developing great leaders is based on the way we respond to life's challenges and obstacles.

How could I count it all joy? Because I chose to trust God and see it from this perspective: I could have been killed, but I had survived the wreck that destroyed my vehicle. Surely God still had a purpose for me and for my family. God saw something that day I couldn't see; He saw my future.

This book is written to anyone and everyone who is not just looking to survive, but is looking to thrive in life. It's written to remind you that God is good and He is, and always will be, the one in control. You can truly trust Him, even when it does not make sense. My intent is that you understand this: God's way of choosing and developing great leaders is based on the way we respond to life's challenges and obstacles.

I later went on to see, and still see every single day, that God will take me through every challenge if I trust Him and turn to Him. My life changed that day in the ditch, with my car wrecked and my future looking pretty much the same. I realized I had the authority to choose the way I would respond to what life would throw at me. Since then, I've discovered that while I will still face sudden challenges, I simply need to hear God before I choose my answer—and I can train myself to respond correctly by the pre-

> **Your plans and visions may map out your course, but your responses or reactions will ultimately define your destination.**

choices I make. Choices like reading God's word daily and prayer. Through Scripture, I can learn how to train my responses to come more naturally; more like a reaction, but based on wisdom that has been gained over time.

Since that day in the ditch, I have seen God bless me and elevate my position of influence within His kingdom. I have learned that the creator of the universe, who calls each of us by name, wants us to aspire to become leaders with influence. He raises leaders every day, but the problem is few of us understand how He does it.

It's time to consider how you will respond to challenges and tough times. When you realize your response can come from somewhere other than just your gut, that you have a better option, then you can focus on where the best response always comes from: God. Your plans and visions may map out your course, but your responses or reactions will ultimately define your destination.

"Now Joseph had a dream, and he told it to his brothers; and they hated him even more. So he said to them, 'Please hear this dream which I have dreamed: There we were, binding sheaves in the field. Then behold, my sheaf arose and also stood upright; and indeed your sheaves stood all around and bowed down to my sheaf.'

And his brothers said to him, 'Shall you indeed reign over us? Or shall you indeed have dominion over us?' So they hated him even more for his dreams and for his words."

Gen. 37:5-8

CHAPTER 2 ↑

THE 1,100 MILE STEP OF FAITH

It dawned on me, after taking in what was left of my vehicle, the insurance company would deem my car totaled. I decided to catch a ride with the tow truck to my house.

As I sat in that truck, the "provider instinct" in me began running through a hundred scenarios. I needed a solution; I was driving to Florida in a week. I called the insurance company, who agreed to cover a rental car for my trip. What would I do for transportation once I had to turn the rental in? We had a second vehicle, an SUV, but our plan was to leave it behind for a friend to sell. It leaked so much water and oil, there was no way to drive it across Dallas—nevertheless more than 1,100 miles back to Florida! I made another quick call to my brother Alan, a mechanic in North Florida, who told me if I could get the car to him he would get it fixed.

That left only one choice: I would drive the rental car and my sixteen-year-old son Hunter would drive our barely-running SUV behind me.

I'm sure it was an adventure for him as we packed the truck with both oil and water; we fully expected it to leak so badly we'd have to stop at every do-it-yourself car wash along the way and wash off the undercarriage to keep it from catching on fire. We even prayed over the vehicle before we left, asking God to help us make it and keep us safe along the way.

Can you recall times when God has been with you through it all? When cloud-filled storms were held in check, and the peace of the living God transcended all understanding? Somehow you were sustained with unending satisfaction in the very core of your being. Perhaps it was a miracle in the ordinary, or a miracle that changed the course of your life forever.

Whether that moment was a miracle of healing, answered prayer, deliverance, or financial breakthrough, I am convinced those miracles are the sovereign outcome of when an invisible God does something in a visible world. I call those times "E.T." moments. I don't mean extra-terrestrial, but "eternity-time": that moment when eternity touches time. Those unexpected bursts of joy when you desperately need some relief are the moments when the unseen power of the eternal God reaches down to touch you exactly where you are. For a split second, an ordinary occurrence becomes a holy collision between eternity and the everyday.

We saw our own eternity-time moment as my son drove our SUV home. More than nine hundred miles later, my son and I were firsthand partakers of a miracle when we arrived safely in Marianna, Florida. As we pulled up to my brother's house with our worn-out vehicle, we had the same amount of oil and water we had when we left Texas. Mile after mile, we never lost any fluids, nor did the vehicle ever overheat. To this day, we can only say that God stuck His finger somewhere inside of our wounded SUV and made a way for us to get to Florida. My brother was amazed that we drove it that far without complications.

When you are hurting and under attack, nothing removes your fear faster than seeing God's hand at work in a specific area in your life. The smallest ounce of faith can sprout into a tree, great and tall, from hearing God's word and witnessing His power. To get strength, we simply have to look at the little, intricate everyday miracles.

That leads us to the question: How do you experience a miracle? The key is this: you have to be in a position to need one. You must step out onto unsure steps and wait for God to catch you. The enemy wants you to play it safe, but when God has called you, you need to step out and take risks, and trust the catcher of your soul to produce your miracle.

Once I arrived at my brother's house, the plan was to leave Hunter with him to help fix the car while I went to Orlando to meet up with Tracee and begin the job-hunting process.

I was about to leave when my brother's pastor stopped by for a surprise visit. Pastor Jeff and I had known each other for quite a while, but it had been a long time since we'd seen each other. Pastor Jeff was eager to hear what God was doing in our lives and ministry. I gave him the short version of our adventures since going to Dallas and how we were now returning in faith to plant a church. He asked me if I would stay in town to attend the service that night, which I declined because I really needed to hit the road and get to Orlando. However, he persisted until I finally agreed to stay.

It was a wonderful service, and you could feel the love of God throughout. Pastor Jeff asked me to share with the congregation what God had done for us by getting the car from Dallas to Florida. Afterwards, he surprised me by taking up an offering. He wanted to sow into us and the new work God was calling us to do.

I couldn't believe it! The amount of the check was exactly what we needed to rent a house Tracee found earlier that week. I was in awe of the miracles I was seeing right in front of me. God had gotten our vehicle home to be repaired by my brother, and now his pastor had taken up a large enough offering to get us into a house for at least a month.

You've heard the phrase "you can't walk on water unless you are willing to get out of the boat." Well, I believe you can't walk on water unless you are first willing to climb *into the boat* that is headed out to the deepest parts of the water—where water-walkers walk best!

From that time, we've seen God do miracle after miracle in our lives, and I'll share more of those throughout the book. As huge and "on time" as those miracles were, they are not the greatest ones we've seen since that leap of faith over ten years ago. At the mention of the totaled car, and God's command to choose joy as my attitude, I am reminded of the other vehicles we were given that same year. In what was a tough test, we lost our main mode of transportation, but God replaced the totaled car when a kind friend blessed me with a vehicle for free—and in that same year, He also provided used vehicles for my wife and our college-aged son through the generosity of others. God saw something I couldn't see when my car was totaled; He saw the blessing He would eventually bring—a blessing worth more than what I originally had.

THE DANCE CARD

Early in this process, God gave me the perfect illustration for a principle He was teaching me. I refer to this as "The Dance Card."

Many years ago, it was a societal custom for girls attending balls or social events to carry a dance card. These cards listed every song to be played, the composer, and whom she intended to dance with. If you've ever heard a guy say to a girl, "Make sure you pencil me into your dance card," that's where it comes from.

In one of my favorite movies, *Meet Me in St. Louis*, there is a very entertaining scene in which two sisters, Esther and Rose, conspire against a rival they think is trying to make a move on one of the sisters' boyfriends. While attending a Christmas ball, they plot to prefill the dance card of their nemesis, Lucille Ballard, with all the worst guys at the ball. However, in a weird turn of fate, they discover Lucille is actually interested in none other than their very own brother.

Little sister Esther ends up honoring the dance card by dancing all the numbers she set up for Lucille. She spends almost the entire night dancing with the most undesirable guys you can imagine, until her grandfather steps in and whisks her away. As grandpa is twirling her across the room, he tells her how proud he is of her for dancing through the dance card instead of trying to avoid it—which leads right into the climax of the movie, when he hands her off to the man of her dreams for the final number.

In life, we are all given a dance card. While we'd love to pre-fill our dance cards with the best experiences, jobs, salaries, relationships, and dreams, it can't be. Some of the dances have already been assigned to partners that we would never choose to trip-the-light-fantastic with. Like Esther in the Bible, we can accept our assignment and choose to dance our way through it, or we can stop dancing altogether.

Great leaders emerge from everyday people who take the dance card they've been given and keep moving their feet. They toe-tap their way through their card, despite the adversity, strife, and darkness. As we've already discussed, Joseph went from being a rejected brother to a world ruler—and the first number on his dance card was the samba of a slave, followed by a fox-trot of being falsely accused. He would later be thrown into jail and forgotten, but eventually he *danced* his way into the palace and became the Prime Minister of Egypt. Great leaders have all had things on their dance card they would've never chosen. Maybe they were born into poverty, had a handicap, or failed in school. No matter what was on their dance card, they kept up a trust-tango with God. They *responded* in a way that prepared them for the next step in leadership. To go from the pit to the palace, you too must learn to dance in the pit before you can dance in the palace.

> **To go from the pit to the palace, you too must learn to dance in the pit before you can dance in the palace.**

So, we have established that the key to God moving us from the pit to the palace is all in how we respond to what life throws at us. I've heard people argue over whether trouble is caused by God, by the devil, or just our own sinfulness. I really don't know the full answer to that question, but I do know the answer to this question: who can use trials, troubles, and even failure to prepare us and propel us into our destiny? Who can take the bitter lemons of our life and turn them into the most magnificent lemonade man has ever dreamed of tasting? God can! If we turn to God and choose to respond up to everything life throws at us, those troubles and trials can become the staircase that leads to greatness. But we've got to be willing to walk the staircase.

THE JOSEPH PATTERN

Are there any patterns in what I experienced? Is there anything I can pass on to others going through trials of their own? I believe applying God's word is the key to everything we experience in life. In the wonderful words of Scripture there are all kinds of truths and promises for us, His children. During some of the darkest times of my journey, well before going to Dallas, I learned how important it is to cling to the word of God; how absolutely vital it is to depend on His sovereignty.

I also believe there are patterns for how God works on behalf of His people in the Bible. When I look within God's word, there is not one story that injects more endless hope than the story of Joseph. My experience parallels his story at points, but on a much smaller scale. While the pattern fits some of my experience, I had never gone through anything quite like Joseph did—he was betrayed by his own *brothers*. He endured a humiliation of a different kind. The truth is, the same God who gave Joseph the strength to endure the worst times of his life is the same God who is with us through ours.

IT ALL BEGINS WITH A DREAM

In the story of Joseph, found in Genesis, we read how it all began: with a dream. How many of your challenges only appeared *after* you discovered your dream? You dream of a new career and take the job you think will ignite your climb up the corporate ladder. The first week is a dream come true, a honeymoon of smooth roads—until it all turns on you. Something happens, your boss gets upset without cause, and you start to discover things about his management style you didn't know when you first took the job.

The question remains the same in every situation: what are you going to do? How are you going to respond to the trial you're going through? You can quit, you can blame others, you can get angry (and stay angry), or go through the motions until you find a way out. Life is not easy, but we need to understand it's God who leads us to these paths—even the uphill, narrow, and winding ones.

Joseph had a dream; in fact, as we'll see later, he had two dreams. From that first dream, Joseph was not celebrated or even encouraged. No, instead he was despised, rejected, and sold into slavery. This was not at the hands of an enemy but from those closest to him; his very own blood. Your dreams will be tested, and sometimes God will use the people closest to you to bring the test.

God had a plan, and that was to raise Joseph up and send him to the second highest political office of the land. The plan of God was to develop Joseph into a great leader who would eventually save His people and many others from starvation. You may think (like I did) that if God wanted to raise Joseph into a great leader, He could have simply taught him what he needed to know and put him in line for the position. God could do that, right? Why didn't He just select the man and put him in the position of power? Why did Joseph need to be sold into slavery, taken to a foreign country, falsely accused, falsely imprisoned, and forgotten by those whom he helped? Why did it take thirteen years of pain, disappointment, and suffering before he was promoted into the second highest position in all of Egypt? It didn't make much sense to me at first;

> Becoming a great leader is all about responding the right way to everything life throws at you, which allows God to shape greatness within your being.

it seemed like a lot of needless suffering. However, we must understand what God says in Isaiah 55:8: "'For My thoughts are not your thoughts, nor are your ways My ways,' says the Lord."

In other words, God knows what He is doing. Even though we do not understand it, we don't always need to. We just need to trust His way works. I believe when God chooses someone for leadership, He still has to teach him or her how to lead. Let me tell you, learning through your own experiences teaches you far better than reading about someone else's. The greatest leaders who've ever lived will admit learning is something they never stop doing. As I stated in the beginning, some leaders are born, but most leaders are made. Joseph was born to lead and save his family, but God had to shape him into the man he needed to be first—and Joseph had his part to do by applying what God taught him. He had to respond correctly, humbly, and reverently in order for God to mold him and transform him into the leader he was destined to become. Becoming a great leader is all about responding the right way to everything life throws at you, which allows God to shape greatness within your being. Sadly, there are too many people who quit in the middle of this boot camp because they lose heart or get discouraged with God and just quit believing.

This pattern of God's uses the hard things of life, the trials and challenges, to suit us up for leadership as found all throughout Scripture. A young David overcame the lion, the bear, and the giant on his way to the throne of Israel. We are tested and tried, but understand this: every obstacle is an opportunity to grow stronger and wiser. The better we respond to tough situations, the more we become like Christ.

The pattern of Joseph's life is directly related to how he responded, as opposed to how he acted. In our lives, we will face some of the same things Joseph faced. How did he respond? There are seven crucial principles we can learn from the patterns crisscrossing Joseph's response.

THE "BIG 7" TEST:

1. Dreams: No matter what Joseph went through on his journey, he never let go of his dream. There is no doubt he showed youth and inexperience by sharing his dreams of future prominence with older brothers who were already jealous of him.

How do *you* respond or react to someone else's dream? When someone tells you about a new idea or goal, do you encourage them or are you like Joseph's brothers—a dream killer? I call Joseph's brothers "first reactors." Their knee-jerk reaction bubbled right up from the emotion of jealousy and envy. In the words of Rick Godwin, "Jealousy digs the mud that envy throws at success."[2] Sadly, there are more dream killers than there are dream chasers. Which one are you? The way we respond to the dreams of others can determine whether we will eventually grow into a leader or not.

2. Rejection: Joseph experienced rejection on a level most of us will never face. He was despised by everyone except his father, and was later left forgotten to rot in prison. He had every reason to lament; to cry the "why me?" cry. Incredibly, he chose instead to respond to rejection in a way that set him apart from others. His unlikely response to desertion and betrayal was a common thread throughout his story.

3. Unwanted Change: Nothing in life is predictable. For Joseph, it was one extreme, unplanned change after another. Change will come, we know that, but Joseph learned how to respond to radical changes the right way. To be an overcomer, we must learn how to respond as he did.

4. Temptation: Nothing has caused more leaders to fail than the trap of temptation. Even the temptation to quit is often a daily battle. We have all seen people destined for great influence lose it all simply because they were overtaken with grief or succumbed to a temptation which destroyed them.

In Joseph's life, he faced several temptations that could have destroyed him. At the time, the manner in which he responded brought more misery, but also kept him in line with God's plan for him. How do we position ourselves to minimize our chances of falling into temptation? It's all in how we respond.

5. Promotion: Eventually every leader will be accorded some type of power or authority. Like temptation, this also can be a test that many would-be leaders fail. How did Joseph handle his position of influence? How did he respond when he was placed in charge at Potiphar's house, the prison, and eventually Pharaoh's palace? Nothing reveals more about a future leader than how they handle power.

6. Waiting: Is there anything harder than waiting for something you really want? Waiting can be difficult at times; however, waiting to get out of something, like prison, is a different experience altogether.

Waiting is the process of letting time go by without getting what we want, and is a great revealer of who we really are. Waiting teaches steadfastness. It's our least favorite professor, but nothing will develop us into great leaders like learning to wait. You can either complain every time life shows you the waiting room or refuse to let it get you down; either way, you still have to wait. Great leaders understand that unnecessary complaining, particularly over something out of their control, accomplishes nothing. In Joseph's story, it's evident that although it took many years for God's dream to come true in his life, he waited the right way.

7. Offense: In life, we can pretty much count on being hurt by others. Even Jesus experienced it through the simple kiss of betrayal delivered by Judas. The most crucial test in Joseph's rise from slave to prime minister was whether he would forgive those who

> **Every test is a door: a door to greatness beyond your current situation or status, or a door to your own prison.**

had hurt him deeply. Every test is a door: a door to greatness beyond your current situation or status, or a door to your own prison. Joseph responded to hurt in a way that foreshadowed the response of Jesus.

In the forthcoming chapters, I'll take you through these individual challenges Joseph faced. Like Joseph, all of us will have to dance our own "dance card of life" and learn how we, like Joseph, can respond up. As we explore his journey—and the stories of other men and women who've followed in his footsteps—I'll unlock his secret keys to promotion and advancement.

"Then he dreamed still another dream and told it to his brothers, and said, 'Look, I have dreamed another dream. And this time, the sun, the moon, and the eleven stars bowed down to me.'

So he told it to his father and his brothers; and his father rebuked him and said to him, 'What is this dream that you have dreamed? Shall your mother and I and your brothers indeed come to bow down to the earth before you?' And his brothers envied him, but his father kept the matter in mind."

Gen. 37:9-11

CHAPTER 3

RESPONDING TO A DREAM

Joseph's journey was catapulted by one thing: a dream.
Although sharing that dream God gave him at first brought
unforeseen misery, he never allowed despair to overrule his
life-guiding principle to trust in God. Scripture doesn't give
us a ton of specific insight into the thoughts of Jacob's sev-
enteen-year-old son, but there are still a great many discoveries, including personal character traits, to be gleaned from
this famous story.

Joseph, as the favorite son of Jacob, always dealt with
jealousy from his older brothers. I can only imagine how tough
they must have been on him early on, for we know they had
grown to hate him even before he shared his dreams. It got
worse for him when he did. In his brother's eyes, until that-
moment Joseph had always been nothing more than an
arrogant "daddy's boy"; now he had delusions of grandeur!

KILLER VS. HANDLER

Consider how Joseph's brothers reacted to his dreams.
Their jealousy grew to the point they sold him as a slave! You
would never do something like that, would you?

Now hold on. Don't answer so quickly.

Take an open and honest look at how you reacted the
last time someone shared a dream with you. When someone
told you about his or her new idea, goal, or ambition, how

did you react? Were you a "Dream Killer" or were you a "Dream Handler"?

What language did you use?

Dream Killer Language:

- You're not ready...
- Why would you want to...
- I'm a true friend, so I have to tell you that...
- Are you crazy?!
- But what about...
- That's not you...
- I'm going to save you from embarrassing yourself...
- Who do you think you are?
- There's no money in that...
- This is going to end in, "I told you so..."
- You're too old to...
- You don't have enough experience to...
- It will never work...

There is an endless list of how friends and so-called supporters *"keep it real."*

Unfortunately, there are far more Dream Killers out there than Dream Handlers. Dream Killers can't see themselves as more than what they are, and they project their inabilities and self-imposed limitations on others. They will most likely never start their own business, further their education, or step into any uncharted water. Because they can't see themselves taking a risk and doing something new, they don't want anyone around them to do anything out-of-the-box either.

You must understand this: when someone asks for your advice or tells you their dream, you are in a position of authority. We have the power to wield life and death with the very words that come out of our mouths, right? What will you speak into that person's dream? The choice is yours. In case you were wondering, it is from the many faces of jealousy and fear that the Dream Killer vocabulary flows.

That's why I praise God for Dream Handlers! Encouragers. People who don't look at someone's situation, but instead look at the direction in which that person is headed. Sure, they might see roadblocks, they might see signs of caution, but they also see the favor of

> **Great leaders don't just give birth to their own dreams, they also act as holy deliverers for the dreams of others.**

the Lord on the life of each person who serves and trusts Him. Instead of feeding negativity into a vision, they brainstorm alongside the dreamer, providing wisdom, solutions, and most of all...hope.

I am not going to ask which one you have been. What you were in the past is dead. I just ask you now: from this day forward, which one will you be?

The way we respond to the dreams others share with us and the dreams we have for our lives will determine if God eventually molds us into leaders. Great leaders don't just give birth to their own dreams, they also act as holy deliverers for the dreams of others.

HOW DO YOU DEAL WITH YOUR OWN DREAMS?

Every leader has a desire within him or her to do something, be something, and stand for something. Do you hang onto to those hopes, undeterred by what others think? Will you let God guide you to His desired outcome? Will you continue your pursuit even when you realize that in God's plan, your dream's ending will not be about you, but will always point to His glory?

How can the way you respond to a dream be so important? In order to understand the answer to that question, you need to first understand exactly what a dream is.

There are two ways in which we generally define what a dream really is. Some define a dream as something that occurs during sleep, as the result of subconscious activity taking over in the brain as conscious activity decreases or stops. These visions and images are almost like a movie, telling a story.

A dream can also be the relentless burn of a desire within you: a vision of the destiny you long for, so clear that you can literally taste it. It is from these dreamers that we derive the term "visionary," to describe someone who envisions a predetermined outcome or path. In this context, dreaming is the thread that weaves the fabric of achieving a goal.

We each carry two types of dreams: those implanted in us by God, and those we've conjured up for ourselves. I believe Joseph's dream had a little bit of both. On one hand, it was a vision given to him by God. On the other hand, it was an inward desire most likely born out of his birth rank

44

as youngest brother: his innate desire to be accepted and appreciated by his family.

Everyone dreams, but not everyone responds correctly to the dreams they dream. Many theologians and teachers have stated Joseph should have never shared his dream with his brothers. It seems like an immature decision to just spill to your older brothers that you have a premonition you will one day rule over them.

Maybe it was premature, but if what Joseph shared with his siblings was the outcome of a holy hint sent straight from God, then the end result testified to his dream's prophetic validity. Sure, Joseph had to endure many trials and tribulations, but in time his vision became a reality.

Then again, maybe it can serve as a good lesson for us to be careful what we share—and with whom. We all know the end of the story reveals that, even if Joseph made mistakes of character, judgment, and wisdom along the way, if God is involved and we grant Him the control of our lives, He will work it all out for the good of those who love Him.

How did Joseph respond to his dream, and what we can learn about responding to our own? There are two things to take home from Joseph's response:

Joseph was open to dreaming! While that response can be questioned, let's not miss the most important response that Joseph had to the dreams. He was open to them. He didn't let his youth or position shut them down.

The most important response to any God-granted dream or desire is: are you open to it? Are you open to even thinking it could be true? Sadly, the truth is there are many Josephs

45

who can't even take the first step of their God-given destiny because they are simply not open to believing in it.

Growing up, I was very blessed in the fact that I had incredible parents who never discouraged me from dreaming. Both of my parents encouraged me to be my best at whatever I did; I don't ever remember one of them telling me I would fail at something. I am sure they gave me a lot of guidance and tried to steer me from things that were not in my best interest, but they never tried to kill or destroy one of my dreams.

Unfortunately, not everyone has the type of parents I have. Some people have grown up in an environment that is poisonous for dreaming. I had a friend who lived in a house like that. As soon as he brought up the idea of something he wanted to try, or someone he'd like to become, there was always a member of his family who'd bring him back down to earth with a comment like: "you will never be that," or "you need to stop dreaming and live in the real world," and "you will never make it."

After many years of comments like that, a person learns not to share his dreams with anyone—and also not to even open up to a dream. They just stop dreaming. They give up. They don't even consider the possibility of making their heart's visions come true. What a sad way to waste a life that, under different circumstances and motivating factors, could have realized the purpose for which he or she was created.

Joseph never gave up on his dream! I think of Joseph and all he endured, even before he was thrown into the pit and sold as a slave. In Genesis 37:4 it states, "But his brothers hated Joseph because their father loved him more than the rest of them. They couldn't say a kind word to him" (NLT). In other words, they had always been Dream Killers. How was it that Joseph, born into a house full of Dream Killers, could be open to a vision from God? What kept Joseph from turning out like others who have been abused and despised by their own family?

He continued to pursue his destiny until the end. He instinctively knew there was an outcome bigger than what he could ever imagine if he persisted in being obedient and faithful to God. For his faith and perseverance, Joseph was granted the privilege of witnessing his vision unfold into a physically manifested destiny.

What else did Joseph consistently do in response to every dream he had?

1. He identified the dream

Not every dream we dream comes from God, but taking the time to learn to discern will develop and grow you as a leader and a follower of Christ. Joseph had such a vivid grasp on his dreams that even if he didn't understand the full meaning at that point in his life, he continued to develop his ability to interpret and understand the difference between the dreams God gave him and others.

Just like dreams we dream at night, the day-dreams of our heart need to be sifted and understood. The process not only matures us, but causes us to seek and follow God for wisdom and understanding. As I look back at my life, I can identify times God sparked a dream within my own heart; many times it was the subsequent act of seeking understanding that really changed me. It's worth the time it takes to identify and understand them.

2. He didn't try to make the dream happen in his own strength

Can you imagine Joseph trying to make his brothers bow down to him? Talk about missing the plan of God. While Joseph was not in control of his circumstances after he was sold into slavery, it is clear he wasn't trying to make the dream happen in his own strength. We can never completely make a God-given dream come true through our own plans and effort. Even if it does involve our own planning, it can still take a different path and timetable than what we would have chosen.

Many are the stories of world leaders or famous businessmen and women who dreamed of leadership but almost missed the mark because they tried to make it happen all by themselves—or they just weren't on God's timetable to begin with. Abraham Lincoln is a great example of someone who pursued the dream God had given him, but it didn't happen when he wanted or the way he first wanted it to. God chooses the roads that lead to our future and the fulfillment of dreams He gives us. No one can get there on his or her own.

How should we view our dream if our aim is to be armed with a "best-case response scenario" at every step of the journey?

- Realize **your dream will always look different in the end.** We all visualize the end result of our dream—but we're limited by the extent of our imagination. And that is good. Our imagination has led us to accomplish great tasks, dream big dreams, and achieve astonishing feats of innovation and invention in all areas of our human experience, but when God's imagination is applied to it as well, it will always look different in the end.

- Realize **God-given dreams almost always end up bigger than they are right now.** No matter how hard we try, even in our wildest dreams, we can never out-dream God. Just remember, God dreamed everything into existence. He is the ultimate creative being. He is the creator.

- Realize **every dream God gives us is ultimately about others, and for His glory.** Not one of our dreams has ever been able to surpass the magnitude, scope, and purpose of God's dream. As it comes to fruition, it will do so to bless us and others; to accomplish that for which it was intended according to His plan.

If we are able to realize the magnitude of God's perfect will in seeing our dream become a reality, we will then be empowered to passionately pursue it. Knowing that it's a God-given ambition to begin with, we can let go of the outcome since God will be orchestrating our steps to the end.

49

"Joseph went after his brothers and found them in Dothan.

Now when they saw him afar off, even before he came near them, they conspired against him to kill him. Then they said to one another, 'Look, this dreamer is coming! Come therefore, let us now kill him and cast him into some pit; and we shall say, "Some wild beast has devoured him." We shall see what will become of his dreams!'

So it came to pass, when Joseph had come to his brothers, that they stripped Joseph of his tunic, the tunic of many colors that was on him. Then they took him and cast him into a pit. And the pit was empty; there was no water in it.

And they sat down to eat a meal. Then they lifted their eyes and looked, and there was a company of Ishmaelites, coming from Gilead with their camels...So Judah said to his brothers, 'What profit is there if we kill our brother and conceal his blood? Come and let us sell him to the Ishmaelites, and let not our hand be upon him, for he is our brother and our flesh.' And his brothers listened. Then Midianite traders passed by; so the brothers pulled Joseph up and lifted him out of the pit, and sold him to the Ishmaelites for twenty shekels of silver. And they took Joseph to Egypt."

Gen. 37:17-20, 23-28

CHAPTER 4

RESPONDING TO REJECTION

Have you ever felt rejected? Of course you have. We have all experi-enced the pain of being turned down, turned away, left alone or forgotten. The residue of rejection can often linger for months, years, or decades, and if not monitored, into the lives of our children—our legacy. It is a mighty tool that the enemy of your soul uses to keep you away from the will of God.

While studying for this book, I realized the feeling of rejection comes in two parts. The first is the sting of instant pain, when you feel the inner pain, right in your gut, of being rejected—or worse, betrayed. An inner pang of disappointment sits right down in the very place where an expectant hopefulness was sitting just moments before. It's usually accompanied by a hot flash around your face and neck, and a cold, numbing feeling in the pit of your stomach. It's a terrible few moments or even minutes. The sudden, unwelcome entrance of disappointment is not fun; however, that pain is just the left jab before the jaw-breaking right hook.

The second pain—the really troubling one—comes from the crystal clear message sent by an individual or a group that you are not wanted. You are not good enough. The "oh yeah, that one is trouble." This is the pain that takes the momentary embarrassment, puts it in a meat grinder, squeezes out all of the juices (the reasonable truth) from it, and creates something ugly and devastating.

You hear this pain manifest itself in the way many people around you talk and the way they act; it is the reason why there is such division in the world, even in the church. It's the reason for divorce, brothers getting into fights, sisters not talking to each other, defaming of pastors, and more. One dark meeting with rejection has the potential to ruin a life forever.

One of the other friends whom rejection brings to the party is loneliness. Loneliness gets invited because we don't like to tell people when we've been rejected; it's embarrassing. So we internalize it ourselves and cut off all outlets for it. It's part of the reason why so many people are aloof and loners today.

As you have no doubt experienced, there are leaders whom you've liked, shall we say, "more than others." This world is not absent of bad leaders who are hurting people. I cringe when I think of the harm and devastation I've seen injurious leaders cause. There are so many people today harboring resentments from rejection and, whether intentionally or not, they spread their negativity around like a plague, infesting those whose immune systems aren't strong enough to withstand it. I want you to understand this: your response to rejection will determine where you end up. You will either become a master builder or a devastating destroyer.

> I want you to understand this: your response to rejection will determine where you end up. You will either become a master builder or a devastating destroyer.

Joseph had more rejection than any one person should ever have, but yet he turned out to be a great leader. Despite being ripped from his family, being sold and falsely imprisoned, he eventually saved his family—those that harmed him. In all probability, he also saved the eventual seed of Abraham, the father of our faith!

I have dealt with rejection several times in my life. Each one of those encounters presented an opportunity to become hurt or bitter. I was fortunate to have parents and leaders who not only encouraged me, but provided me with an example to emulate. I watched how they dealt with rejection and learned how to respond instead of react.

When I was younger, I worked as a state trooper for the Florida Highway Patrol. I was known as a hard-working, good-humored guy, but one day I suddenly found myself rejected by some of the people I worked with. I was in one of those situations where my peers began to believe I wasn't a very good employee based on misinformation from another co-worker. The world has a saying: "Sticks and stones may break my bones but words will never hurt me." That is such a lie! Words crush people. In fact, the Bible says we all have the power of life and death through the words that come out of our mouths.

It started when I noticed people acting a little differently toward me. Then one day I woke up and realized I had gone from being the popular, jovial guy everyone talked with to being the guy everyone avoided. While no one came up to my face and directly said nasty things to me—not nearly like the personal, in-your-face attacks Joseph endured—their apparent hostility and unwillingness to strike up conversation with me hurt my heart. That morning, when I fully realized how I was being treated, the rejection penetrated deep into my very soul. It left me with very little strength and energy to dress and go to work.

While we all have to deal with rejection, fortunately for us God has a biblical prescription for healing; some surefire ways to bounce back from a brush-off.

1. **Turn to God**

The pain of rejection Joseph felt was very real—no one could ever go through what he did without feeling utterly unloved. God didn't insulate him from the pain; that's not His way. He knows that although the pain is real, the solution is as well. Although we can't read the thoughts of Joseph during that time in his life, we can easily surmise he turned to God because the Bible states that throughout this process God was with him. God was with him because he was with God. In the first part of James 4:8 it states: "Draw near to God and He will draw near to you."

I find it very interesting that the Bible says, "God was with him." Why? Because God is *always* everywhere, right? He is omnipresent. Of course He was with Joseph. But the Bible gets deeper than that. There is a difference between God's omnipresence and His manifest presence. For Joseph, there was a special presence of God that was riding sidecar with him during those tough times when there was no one else. I love this truth: if God did that for Joseph, He'll do that for you and me.

Too many times people turn the rejections of man into the rejections of God. It is easy to do, but it's wrong. Do not equate the rejection of fallen man with the rejection of God. Men and women let each other down simply because of the imperfect nature of mankind. God's perfect love will never leave us or reject us in this life. We can always turn to Him in our time of need and find help—doing so puts us closer to the path of greatness.

During my time of personal rejection as a state trooper, I, like Joseph, made the decision to turn to God and trust Him. I would love to say it was easy, but it was anything but easy. All I could do was cling to His word and trust He would make things better. I can remember sitting in my car, parked off the road, reflecting on what had occurred. It was also during those quiet times I would find

> **Too many times people turn the rejections of man into the rejections of God.**

the deep part of my soul turning toward God in quiet expectation; expectation that He would speak to me through His word or His Spirit.

2. **Listen to His voice**.

I have found that when I pray to God to make things better, many times He will give me *instruction* instead of just making the problem go away. While He still can and will remove the obstacle, many times He wants me to do something while I am waiting on Him for the eventual deliverance. God typically changes our perspective first—not the situation. Once your perspective aligns to God's ideology, you become the agent of change in the situation.

During my time of testing, I asked God what He wanted me to do. I heard these words in my spirit, "Don, just do your job and be a good trooper."

I seriously wanted Him to change my situation as quickly as possible. A sense of embarrassment and anger threatened to overtake me every time I went to work. I wanted to talk to people, confront them, force them to hear my side, but God had a different plan.

That's not what I wanted. I wanted God to fix it, and fix it quickly and decisively. My very nature wanted to rail against what I knew the Lord was telling me. "Go back to work and don't defend yourself" was not what I wanted to hear. If there is one thing in life that I know to be true, it is the importance of learning to hear the voice of God. Once I had heard it, I had a choice to make: obey Him, or do it my way.

> **I heard these words in my spirit, "Don, just do your job and be a good trooper."**

What are you going through now that you need to hear God's voice on?

3. **Obey His voice.**

Over the next several months I did just what He asked me to do. I went to work and did my job the best way I knew how. I didn't stop there though; I went a little further. I was determined to also be the best co-worker I could, even to those who had rejected me. Sometimes you just need to go a little further.

Do you remember when Jesus sent Simon to go into the water to fish? Jesus didn't tell Simon how far to go into the water. Get this in your spirit: He tells us what to do, but at the end of the day, it's up to us individually to determine how much we are going to try—how far into the water we are going to go.

I mentally prepared myself to go above and beyond what was expected of me. If one of my co-workers was working a bad wreck, I would show up to help them even if I didn't have to. When one of them crossed my path, I greeted them in the same jovial manner I used to. See, I had let their opinions of me change the way I treated them. I decided to be the person they had always known, not the person they had heard about. I asked them about their

> **Rejection causes people to rebel against the people doing the harm, but instead I learned to rebel against the rebellion growing in my heart.**

day, about their golf game, about their children, and everything else as if we were good friends. It wasn't easy to force a smile and try to get some of them to engage in conversation, but I was determined that their hostility towards me was not stronger than my kindness.

Day after day I just kept doing a good job and treating everyone they way He wanted me to treat them. The pain of rejection did not instantly disappear. In fact, it met me at the door to the zone I was working every morning. Rejection causes people to rebel against the people doing the harm, but instead I learned to rebel against the rebellion growing in my heart. God told me to do a good job. His love for me was sufficient for me to do so. His grace was enough to cover their transgressions against me. I actually started to feel a great closeness to Jesus, perhaps because I was sharing something in common with Him. I actually wondered if this was what Joseph felt: rejection from man, but closeness with God. For me, I found the pain of rejection was growing less and less while the peace of His presence was growing stronger and stronger.

4. **Expect a breakthrough.**

After several months of consistently doing the best job I could and treating my co-workers like I'd want to be treated, a breakthrough finally came. The truth about what had been said about me came out and everyone saw I was not who I had been made out to be. In short, God defended me and God fought for me. I didn't have to try to convince anyone of anything. God brought out the truth in His perfect timing. My co-workers were glad to know they had been wrong about me, and some even apologized for the way they treated me.

The conversations also turned to the way I had handled that difficult work situation when just about everybody was against me. By His grace, I was able to show them Christ through my actions and inactions. As time went on, God used my response to their rejection to build a platform of trust and respect. I was able to minister to many of those individuals because of how I handled that situation. I even prayed with several of them to receive Christ. What the enemy meant for harm, God turned for great good. I am so thankful that I turned to God and responded up when I went through my time of rejection.

Sometimes rejection comes as an attack and sometimes it comes as the consequence of our own actions. That's right, sometimes we bring it upon ourselves. Have you ever done something stupid or foolish, and the result of it was that people did not want to be connected to you? Hey, it happens to all of us.

Regardless of what actions brought about the rejection you feel, the solution remains the same. Go to God and seek His will; ask Him what to do. He will answer you or lead you to the answer. Once you know what it is, follow it.

Perhaps you're reading this book and don't know the joy of hearing and following the voice of God. I encourage you to make that your goal. Turn to trusted spiritual leaders like your pastors, ministry leaders, or parents. Seek wise spiritual counsel and soon you will learn to discern the many voices of God—for God talks to us in a myriad of ways. You can always find answers through His written word, the inner voice of the Holy Spirit, through spiritual leaders, through dreams, or through anointed songs. If you simply give the effort, He will make it easy for you to find Him.

5. **Believe that God can use it for your good and for His good.**

While abuse and neglect are the highest levels of rejection anyone could ever experience, there is hope. God has the ability to turn your ashes into something beautiful. If you have one of those unhealed wounds, the hurt is probably as fresh as it ever was and you may not see how anything good could possibly come from it. Turn to God and He will comfort you in a way no one else is able to. Give those feelings, that memory, that terrible time, give it all to the Lord. God will take those burnt ashes and do a miracle with it; He will lighten your heart and give you a new song. In time, you will be able to tell others how He has healed you:

> But as for you, you meant evil against me;
> but God meant it for good, in order to bring
> it about as it is this day, to save many people
> alive. Gen. 50:20

If Joseph would have responded to the rejection with hate and revenge, the ultimate plan of God to save Israel—and all of us—through Jesus may have been aborted. However, God delights in taking what the enemy means for harm and turning it into a glorious ending. Jesus, the author and finisher of our faith, responded up when He faced the ultimate rejection on the cross. By responding upward toward His heavenly father, He was able to love those who had just crucified Him. He even said in Luke 23:34: "Then Jesus said, 'Father, forgive them, for they do not know what they do.' And they divided His garments and cast lots."

"Now the Midianites had sold him in Egypt to Potiphar, an officer of Pharaoh and captain of the guard.

Now Joseph had been taken down to Egypt. And Potiphar, an officer of Pharaoh, captain of the guard, an Egyptian, bought him from the Ishmaelites who had taken him down there. The Lord was with Joseph, and he was a successful man; and he was in the house of his master the Egyptian. And his master saw that the Lord was with him and that the Lord made all he did to prosper in his hand. So Joseph found favor in his sight, and served him. Then he made him overseer of his house, and all that he had he put under his authority. So it was, from the time that he had made him overseer of his house and all that he had, that the Lord blessed the Egyptian's house for Joseph's sake; and the blessing of the Lord was on all that he had in the house and in the field. Thus he left all that he had in Joseph's hand, and he did not know what he had except for the bread which he ate."

Gen. 37:36, 39:1-6

CHAPTER 5 ⬆

RESPONDING TO UNWANTED CHANGE

It does not matter how hard we try; we can plan, scheme, schedule, prepare, plot, arrange, or map it out, but still unexpected circumstances have the master key to enter our world without warning. Oftentimes they are unwanted, unneeded, and untimely events that force us to alter our preset courses. Change, whether we expect it or not, is inevitable. Owning this truth is vital to becoming an overcomer. How we respond to unforeseen changes is what separates people in positions of authority from extraordinary leaders.

When I look at how Joseph went from a nobody to a somebody, I see that it was the dry valleys of unwanted and unplanned changes that defined him. Let's explore his journey.

FROM THE PIT TO THE PALACE

In Genesis 37, Joseph shares his dream with his brothers and they decide to kill him and throw him into a pit. They then change the plan from killing him to abandoning him in a pit, but ultimately decide to sell him to a group of Ishmaelite businessmen who are traveling to Egypt. They sold their own brother for twenty pieces of silver, which meant they would not be guilty of murder and make a little money as well. How low did Joseph feel at this point? He was getting ready to feel even lower.

The Ishmaelite businessmen sell Joseph as a slave, but not just to anyone, to the captain of the bodyguard of Pharaoh: a man named Potiphar.

In Genesis 39, we see that God was with Joseph; he becomes a successful steward in the house of Potiphar. He worked his way up the corporate ladder of Potiphar's house, until Potiphar's wife tried to seduce Joseph. When Joseph refused, she accused *him* of trying to seduce *her*. Her false accusation is believed, though, because she is holding the clothes she ripped off him when he ran away to escape her advances. Now, Joseph is back down the ladder and is thrown into an Egyptian prison. Over time, he is blessed again with God's favor and is promoted to overseeing all his fellow prisoners.

What can be worse than being at the lowest point of your life? Being at your lowest point, getting promoted, and then being kicked back down to your lowest point again. Many people would grumble and say that it would have been better to remain at the bottom all along, but not Joseph.

In Genesis 40, we find Joseph overseeing all of the prisoners. After correctly interrupting the dreams of both the Pharaoh's cupbearer and his baker, he asks the cupbearer, whose future was much brighter than that of the baker, to remember him and speak to Pharaoh about getting him out of prison. His hope was that his service to the cupbearer would lead to his eventual release. While the cupbearer was grateful for the interpretation, he forgot about Joseph's request.

More than two years go by, and Joseph is still in prison. It wasn't until Pharaoh had a dream no one could interrupt that the cupbearer remembered Joseph and informed Pharaoh that he knew someone who could interpret his dreams. Pharaoh sent for Joseph right away.

You have to be wondering: "what will go wrong next?" Every time it looked as if something was going to work out, Joseph found him-self back in the bottom of the barrel. No one, without knowing the end of the story, would predict

> **Sometimes it appears that God's steps up the ladder of success go down instead of up.**

that he was about to go from the prison to being second in charge of Egypt. Sometimes it appears that God's steps up the ladder of success go down instead of up.

In a story that reads like a "feel good" Hollywood movie, Joseph interprets the dream of Pharaoh, is promoted to prime minister, and goes on to save the country and his own family. If you love happy endings, you have to love this story. Do you still believe in happy endings? Life can throw changes at you at every corner, but God has the ability to get you to your destination if you stay in faith and respond up.

In fact, if an actor were to play the role of Joseph in a Broadway play, he would be jumped on backstage after every scene as the wardrobe personnel would have to take him from a regular robe, to a robe of many colors, then the robe would have to be bloodied, just before changing to the garb slaves wore. After that, he'd have to change from what a lowly slave in the house of Potiphar would wear into what the most respected slave in Potiphar's house would wear. Once Potiphar's wife ripped that garment off, he'd have to run off stage and emerge in the black-and-white stripes of a prisoner—and for the final number, he'd don the clothes only a prince of Egypt would wear.

Joseph did more than survive in each garment, he did more than just go-with-the-flow; he thrived. Those who respond well thrive well. What was Joseph made of that enabled him to thrive after all of the backstabbing and lies against him?

I want you to take a moment and do a mental review of the last year of your life. Like Joseph, I'm sure you had some unwanted changes. You might've even had some in the past week. Did you not get the promotion you thought you deserved? Did you lose your job? Did you find yourself in the same position I was in, with a totaled car? Worse yet, did you get news from your doctor that no one ever wants to hear? The toughest things in life to respond to are unwanted and unplanned events.

> **Those who respond well thrive well.**

Just a few years ago, Tracee and I planted our first church in Central Florida. We arranged with a local high school to hold our services there. We quickly embraced the school and volunteered to do things such as cook for the football team before their Friday night games. The school became our mission field, and we found ourselves working to help raise money for students who were homeless or had financial needs. We loved the staff and the students; we were all in! I even served the football program by helping to coach the freshman team. I had coached high school football before, so it was easy for me to plug in and help. Not only did I thoroughly enjoy it, but it also helped us get very well connected with the school. I also had a key member of our church help as an assistant coach as well, and both of us became an integral part of the sports program. It was a golden age of several years of peace and influence for our church within the school. It was really where I wanted to spend my life serving God and the community.

Many people are under the misconception that pastors make a lot of money. Some do; however, most don't—especially those pastoring a new church. I had been given a lot of support in the beginning, but three years into our plant, I needed to find a way to supplement my income. It was at that time the sky seemed to part: the principal invited me to come work at the school. The staff and student body truly loved having us, and the opening was for someone who could do some teaching but whose primary role was security. My time as a state trooper and my role as a coach on the football team made me the perfect fit. It seemed like a dream come true; an answered prayer.

The position wasn't available yet. As the date got closer for me to apply, the principal reminded me to keep checking the job listing board, but in the event I missed it, he would also personally check to make sure I knew the position was officially open. My wife and I were happy, as were the other coaches on staff whom I had gotten close to. They felt that the entire school would benefit from me taking that job.

I was at a men's retreat one weekend when the principal called me to tell me the position became available. The organizers of the retreat had asked everyone to give up their cell phones so that we could concentrate on hearing God's voice, so I wasn't able to answer the call Friday evening. We got our phones back on Sunday, and as I went through my voicemails I heard the one left to me by the principal.

"Don, the position you've been waiting for is available. Make sure you apply as soon as possible."

I can still remember the feeling I had on the ride home from the retreat center. I had put in my time, put my finances up in prayer before the Lord, and the principal of the school had called me to make sure I applied. Life was good; although my family had gone through some lean times, everything was finally working out. I was beyond excited!

I got home and shared with my wife stories from the wonderful weekend I had in the presence of God. We talked about the words spoken during the retreat and how blessed I had been to be there. I also shared with her the good news about the job we had been waiting for. I went online that evening to apply—a formality to be sure—however as I searched the website, I found every other job except the one I was looking for. I turned off the computer and figured, it being a Sunday, I would have to wait until Monday morning to talk to the principal and apply then. A part of me figured they didn't even advertise the position since they already knew who they were going to hire.

The following morning I stopped by the principal's office and informed him I couldn't find the job online. I could immediately tell by his countenance something was wrong.

"You did put in for it on Friday, didn't you?" he asked.

"No, I just got your message yesterday. I was at a church retreat."

He took in a deep breath and let out a sigh, "Well, I'm sorry, but I have bad news for you then. Someone else applied for the job and the position has been closed. I called you to let you know and all weekend I thought it was you."

Have you ever had that sinking feeling when you know something is true, but you try to reason a way that it's not real? That's how I felt.

"Is there any way I could go directly to the main office, or is there anyone you can talk to?" I asked. After all, he was the principal and it was a position in his school; if anyone could do something about it, surely he could.

I couldn't wrap my head around the fact I could lose out on my dream job while at a men's retreat where I had felt the favor of the Lord so strongly upon my life. There had to be a way around it, because I just knew this was God's perfect fit for me to reach the school and the community. Unlike other churches who start at a school and leave to get their own building as soon as they get enough money, we actually wanted to stay and grow there. I had overcome obstacles to become the pastor at that school and this latest test had to be the devil trying to destroy God's plan for me and our church. When our perfect plan comes to an end, it's not always the devil's fault, sometimes it is designed by God.

For the next few days I did everything in my power to get the position that my wife, church, and friends at the school knew was meant to be mine. In fact, I had the entire church pray and, once we did, they all thought it would work out. It had to work out; this was the will of God!

I jumped when I got a call from the principal shortly thereafter. He asked me to meet him in his office. I walked into that room full of faith. The only questions I had were: "How did God turn things around, and how am I going to testify about it on Sunday?"

However, the look on his face was similar to the one I had seen before. He told me he was sorry, and it wouldn't have even mattered if I had turned in my resume in time. There was an employee of the school system whose position had been cut at a neighboring school. Because of his tenure, he had first right of refusal. He elected to take the job and there was nothing anyone could do about it. Then he told me there wouldn't be another position like that again for some time, maybe years. I was devastated.

> When our perfect plan comes to an end, it's not always the devil's fault, sometimes it is designed by God.

It seemed to me as if all color died for a moment. I accepted the reality of what had happened, but I struggled with *why* it had happened.

To be clear, this job was not, in any way, going to make my family rich. In reality, I could probably make more money somewhere else. I wanted it so badly because I felt it was the best place to be in order to do God's work. I couldn't understand why God didn't allow me to get that job. Was this God's will, or was it an attack of the enemy?

At about that time Ted Jones, a good friend and the athletic director at the school, spoke to me and told me that it seemed that God was directing me away from working at the school. He went through everything that happened to keep me from even putting in for the position.

"Then what I am supposed to do, Ted?" I asked. My head was in my hands as I sat in his office.

"I don't have the answer, Don, but I wouldn't be surprised if God has something better for you. There is something in this that, if you truly trust Him, will lead to something even better."

We've all had those times when someone is handing us truth on a platter but we are so dejected we simply do not want to hear it. As time went on, I realized God was in that unplanned and unwanted change. It takes time to see the full picture God is painting, and as with any artist, it is so easy to judge it prematurely, especially when the first layers don't look like we expected them to.

The job God had in store for me was a dream come true: working in the Christian book publishing industry. I would never be where I am today, never have written this book you are reading, if God hadn't stepped into that situation and closed the door on me. I have been honored to help thousands of true believers impact the world through their books. I am awed that God put me in a position to shepherd people with a burning desire to share their testimonies, faith, and inspiration through the written word. As a facilitator, I have helped God reach people all over the globe, and not just in a local suburb, as I would have at the school.

God will stop your plan when it's time to start His.

WHAT REACTIONS LOOK LIKE

Let's talk about the term "react." Many define reaction as the impulsive behavior in a certain situation. It is the manifestation to a surprise occurrence.

When you are two hundred feet from a traffic light and it turns from green to yellow, then from yellow to red, what do you do? Do you slow down and come to a complete stop? That's not a reaction. That is a learned behavior. That is a developed response. Don't misconstrue the two.

> God will stop your plan when it's time to start His.

A reaction is what occurs when you are driving on the highway and a deer suddenly crosses your path. Natural instincts take over: the instinct to avoid killing a deer or damaging your new car.

But not all of our instincts are correct or the best choices. Remember Cain? He'll always be remembered as the son of Adam and Eve who reacted in anger and killed his brother Abel because he was jealous that the Lord accepted Abel's gift but not his own. We have a fallen nature; outside of the grace and influence of God, we all posses the ability to react like Cain, even if it's only in our heart.

What do you do when someone insults you in front of your peers? Do you react or respond? How do you behave when you've been unfairly fired from a job without warning? How do you respond to prejudice, racism, or physical violence?

The hidden key is to learn that God uses unplanned things in life to morph our fallen reactions into wise responses. Sure, we will always be tempted to react instead of responding, but if we remain humble and teachable, God will transform us into "first responders" instead of "first reactors."

As I studied the life of Joseph, I see a pattern he displayed consistently. The Bible doesn't get into his inner thoughts, however, by reading between the lines and by seeing what the Bible does say about his character, we can learn these two simple steps to responding the way God wants us to when we experience unwanted or unplanned change.

1. **Don't worry about the things you can't change**. Joseph could do nothing about being sold into slavery. I am sure he was filled with fear and was distraught. However, he trusted in the Lord of hosts, and ultimately he was sold into a "good" situation.

2. **Impact the things you can change.** Some people read the first step and think it means they should worry about the things they can change. That's not what I mean, at all. *Impact* the things you can change. If you can change it, do the necessary things to change

it. Don't cry over something that is in your influence to alter, do that thing you need to do to alter it! Joseph got sold into slavery, but then, when he arrived at Potiphar's house, he worked his way up to being the most valued servant of the estate. God can only bless our work, not our excuses.

When I found out that I was not going to get the job at the high school, I had to accept that I could not change it. The only thing I could control was my attitude about it and my willingness to seek God for my next move. That's what I worked on, getting over my past and pressing into my future.

A LESSON FROM SPACE

I love the story of Apollo 13, which was immortalized in the movie starring Tom Hanks. It details how NASA employees rescued three astronauts from certain death in outer space.

> God can only bless our work, not our excuses.

As the story goes, the space ship, Apollo 13, was put in peril when someone in the command center back in Houston called for them to stir the hydrogen tanks. It was a routine yet necessary maneuver performed on previous missions, always without a problem.

Unknown to Jim Lovell (played by Tom Hanks in the movie) and his team, there was a problem with the wiring. When Jack Swigert (played by Kevin Bacon) stirred the tanks, an explosion occurred that endangered not just the mission but also their lives.

Can you imagine being over two hundred thousand miles away from earth and anyone who could possibly help you? Or, that the ship which protects your very life has been damaged so badly that making it home alive is highly unlikely? It was certainly an unwanted chain of events the three astronauts and the folks at NASA had not anticipated. There were no contingencies for the challenges they faced. Making it back to earth alive was almost inconceivable.

In the movie, we see the good folks at NASA work around the clock as they discover that resolving one problem created another one. Gene Kranz, NASA Flight Director, played by Ed Harris in the movie, is best known by his famous quote, "Failure is not an option." In a telling interview, he provided very insightful information about the three men chosen to crew the Apollo. While many people believed astronauts needed to be engineers or scientists who understood every part of the spacecraft and the moon, Gene wasn't one of them. Gene felt the perfect first astronauts would be military test pilots.

"Experimental" is a good word to describe the type of aircraft test pilots fly. After all of the analysis and theories are done and an aircraft is built, someone has to test it out. Someone has to be the first person to get into the cockpit and make sure the thing even flies. If it does, the pilot must coolly deal with whatever problems or malfunctions that can—and will—occur miles above the ground. A test pilot's main function, besides staying alive, is to gauge how well the aircraft performs according to the specifications of the manufacturer.

Gene understood the benefit of having scientists land on the moon, or the advantage of putting the ship in the hands of an engineer who knew every inch of it; however, even with all of their education and training, he didn't know how well they would handle themselves when the pressure came. Pressure does strange things to people. He couldn't trust them to perform admirably if everything that was supposed to go right went wrong. He needed people who knew how to handle unplanned and unwanted circumstances.

There are times when faith gets tested. Times when someone considers giving up, losing hope, losing composure. Gene wanted experienced test pilots who, even under the threat of losing their own lives, would follow protocol and stay calm. The way they responded to unforeseen circumstances would dictate whether the mission was a success or a colossal failure. The truth was, even though they faced possible death in space, those men responded in a way we all wish we could. They may not have been great leaders when they boarded that spacecraft, but they sure were when they returned. Why? Because of *how* they *responded* to adversity and unwanted and unplanned change.

On the fortieth anniversary of the Apollo 13 mission, I saw an interview by Matt Lauer on *The Today Show* with the real Gene Kranz. The interview played actual video footage taken from inside the cockpit, while Matt and Gene discussed how calm the astronauts were. As Matt Lauer asked Gene Kranz if the astronauts seemed abnormally calm to him, you could tell what a really big deal it was, the way they stayed calm during a crisis.

The reason why Matt asked if they seemed *abnormally* calm was because the men were reporting issues that were, in all likelihood, death sentences for them. Yet, their voices were measured and without much emotion, as if it was just another day at the office.

The wonderful news is that as followers of Christ, we have the same ability to handle adversity as these great men did; in fact, we may have an added advantage. The living God who parted the Red Sea, made the cripple walk, and resurrected Lazarus from the grave is able to help us, but we have to learn how to respond instead of react.

Your response to those moments when life gets tough should not be to run and tell everyone how unfair your life is. God's children are not meant to be woe-is-me-type people. God's people are meant to understand that we can count it all joy when we are faced with unwanted or unplanned change. We know that although the situation looks grim, we serve a very big God who provides, protects, and nourishes us. Our responses have to manifest from the makeup of who we are.

Joseph could have never imagined the many challenges that would come to him through unwanted or unplanned change: being rejected by his brothers, being sold into slavery, being falsely accused, being thrown into jail, being forgotten in jail.

GOD'S PROTECTION CHANGES EVERYTHING

A few years after Tracee and I were married, I was still struggling to find my career. Following good advice, I tried to pursue the path of becoming a loan officer at a local bank. Without the proper experience though, it didn't work out for me. Yet, I felt that I wanted to be in finance. After a lot of searching, I finally landed a position as a manager-in-training for a finance company. I took it because, in time, that position would give me the experience I needed to go back to the bank and apply as a loan officer.

It took less than two months for me to discover that manager/trainee was a fancy title for what I was really doing: collections. It became clear to me that I didn't want to work there anymore. However, I had a family to support so I continued to work hard, despite knowing that it wasn't for me.

After nine months on the job, my manager asked me to go to lunch with him. During lunch, he told me he had concerns for me regarding the position. I showed up on time, I was consistent, and I did my work. However, he still had... *concerns*. The position I held was important to the company because they wanted to train someone who could take over a location one day. I had no intention of running my own location; I didn't even like my day-to-day. I made the decision then and there that I would leave. We parted ways as friends, and as we left the restaurant he told me how bright and adept I was. He even complimented me on my work ethic and said I could use him as a reference.

I will never forget leaving that meeting, knowing I would have to stop at a pay phone to call my wife and tell her I no longer had a job. I couldn't bear to hear the disappointment in her voice. We thought the worst was behind us since I finally had a job with a future. To make matters worse, Tracee was a stay-at-home mom to our one very young daughter with another child on the way.

When I called Tracee, I promised her I would find another job before I got home that evening. I did just what I promised her. I found three part-time jobs: one digging foundations, another tying steel, and the last one was bagging groceries on weekends. Collectively, all three would pay our bills until something else worked out. When I came home, dismissed from one job but with three new ones, Tracee was relieved. If you are a married man, you know how amazing it is when your wife trusts you and feels that you've come through. Sometimes the way we need to respond to losing our job is to keep our faith but start looking for the next one.

About a month later, she and I were watching TV when a report came across the evening news. It was a local network and the story was about a young man who had been shot and killed while working to make a collection for a finance company. I leaned closer to the television, fully engrossed in the story. When the news reporter said the name of the company, I fell back to the cushions with my head tilted back and my hands over my mouth. It was the same company I had just left. A moment later, as the reporter continued to tell the story, I realized that the young man who had been shot to death was the person who was hired to replace me!

I had been so upset when my plans for a full-time job in finance didn't work out. Every day, I reported to my three part-time jobs—each one difficult in its own right—struggling to make up the difference in pay. I couldn't believe that such was my life. Once I saw how I had been protected, though, I was grateful for what God had just done. Each of those part-time jobs was really God's personal signature on my life; He was signing off that I was not only provided for, but protected. The door to my finance job may have been shut, but that doorknob now bore the distinct fingerprints of angelic protection.

> The door to my finance job may have been shut, but that doorknob now bore the distinct fingerprints of angelic protection.

Remember, God can take any situation, even one intended to be bad for us, and oversee a righteous remodel to turn it out for our good. How we respond to unplanned situations is important because we can't see everything, and sometimes, if not most times, God is the one commanding the change.

I rejoice in Him, because He changed my plans that day and sent me out to find those other jobs. That action kept me alive. On top of that, one day while working the job I liked the least—bagging groceries—I met the man who opened the door to my favorite job from that season of my life: coaching football in a successful high school program. It was part time and only lasted a few years, but it is one of the best memories of my adult life. As the Bible says:

> There are many plans in a man's heart, Nevertheless the LORD's counsel—that will stand. Prov. 19:21

I am thankful for this promise in Scripture. I am personally a witness to what the Lord can do when you put yourself in His capable hands. God is sovereign, and I want you to take courage: no matter what circumstance you face right now, God has something better in store for you. Something that will make an even bigger impact for His will here on earth.

Joseph discovered that the way he handled the unwanted changes forced upon him not only led him to a place where he could impact his generation, but save his entire family.

"Now Joseph was handsome in form and appearance.

And it came to pass after these things that his master's wife cast longing eyes on Joseph, and she said, 'Lie with me.'

But he refused and said to his master's wife, 'Look, my master does not know what is with me in the house, and he has committed all that he has to my hand. There is no one greater in this house than I, nor has he kept back anything from me but you, because you are his wife. How then can I do this great wickedness, and sin against God?'

But it happened about this time, when Joseph went into the house to do his work, and none of the men of the house was inside, that she caught him by his garment, saying, 'Lie with me.' But he left his garment in her hand, and fled and ran outside."

Gen. 39:6-9,11-12

CHAPTER 6

RESPONDING TO TEMPTATION

Throughout his life, Joseph was forced to learn how to respond to trials, obstacles, and challenges. Of all of those items he faced, none was more difficult than overcoming the obstacle of temptation. In one of the strongest scenes from the story of his life, we see young Joseph rise to power within the house of his master Potiphar. As he gained the attention of his master, who promoted him to be over every- thing he owned, he also gained the attention of his master's wife. Scripture is clear that Joseph was handsome, and when you add to that his rise in authority, he obviously became very attractive.

One can only imagine what that was like for Joseph; the pressure of that moment had to be immense. I mean, being pursued by your boss's wife? Even if you avoided the situa- tion, there would inevitably come a day when no one was around but you and her and she'd think, "Today there is no one around to catch us, this is my chance to have my way with him."

Even as I begin this chapter, I am conscious of the many people who fall to so many different kinds of temptation on a weekly and even a daily basis. I, like every other human being, have fallen into temptation myself and thankfully Christ's forgiveness was there to wash me and restore me. I know "sin is sin" and we are not supposed to rank them, but honestly there seems to be a big difference between the consequences of falling to temptation to overeat (which I am so guilty of) and falling to the temptation of committing adultery or murder. Sin is sin, and it has a way of destroying your life and future all at once or very, very slowly if it goes unchecked.

While we can't rank sin, I think we can agree there are some mistakes that have the potential to severely damage or end any opportunity of a real future as one of God's greatest leaders. Yes, God can use anyone after they fall; just look at the life of David. However, I doubt very seriously that David would have fallen into the arms of Bathsheba if he had been shown the toll it would take on his legacy, his kingdom, and his children. My point in this chapter is for us to learn anything and everything we can to hopefully avoid falling into any temptations at all—but especially those that lead to such destruction and loss. The good news is, while we can be forgiven for falling, we can also learn how to overcome temptation, especially when it comes to the most destructive sins. My prayer is "Lord, help me to overcome every temptation and live victorious in your power."

It is clear that Joseph didn't commit adultery with his master's wife but instead fled the house as fast as he could. Scripture makes it clear: he left so quickly she was left with his garment in hand. She then proceeded to falsely claim that he had tried to take advantage of her. His rejection of her beckoning call led to him losing his job and being arrested as well. When I look at this moment of decision—a decision instrumental to his journey into greatness—I am intrigued not by what is in the recorded account, but by what is not recorded. It is what you can't read that really holds the truth of gaining victory over temptation. Yes, none of us will be perfect in this life, but if there is a way to avoid temptations of the highest cost, then I want to know!

What does the word temptation really mean? There are actually two meanings: one is an enticement to sin, while the other one refers to a test or trial. Take the Lord's Prayer, for instance. "Lead us not into temptation" is truly referring to our request to not be led into a trial or test. Remember when Jesus prayed He would not have to drink of the cup before His crucifixion? That was a similar use of the same word we see throughout Scripture referencing a test or trial. The other use, to entice one to sin, is found specifically in scriptures like James 1:13-15:

> Let no one say when he is tempted, "I am tempted by God"; for God cannot be tempted by evil, nor does He Himself tempt anyone. But each one is tempted when he is drawn away by his own desires and enticed. Then, when desire has conceived, it gives birth to sin; and sin, when it is full-grown, brings forth death.

When we are looking at how Joseph responded to temptation, it is important to understand how temptation works in someone's life.

First there must be desire. The Bible makes it clear temptation actually begins within a person's own sinful nature. It doesn't begin from outside of anyone; it actually begins within his or her own heart.

Second, there must be an opportunity to fulfill that desire. Someone who has the inclination to steal must find an opportunity to make that desire a reality; likewise, someone who is struggling with lust must have the means and way to make it a reality. Some people actually hunt for the opportunity; others just find themselves almost stumbling across it instead. Either way, both are born out of the sinful desire, the one living within their own flesh, taking its shot.

How did Joseph overcome temptation? Scripture may not map out his escape route, but we have the ability to look at the person, the circumstances, and the outcome to learn a few things. If these things are true for Joseph, they must be true for us. If Joseph could overcome temptation and stop the plan of the enemy, we can as well.

There are four responses to temptation:

1. Recognition
2. Resistance
3. Reasoning
4. Removal

Recognition. The first step to overcoming something is the ability to see it.

> A prudent man foresees evil and hides himself, but the simple pass on and are punished. Prov. 22:3

Sometimes the greatest strength is really recognizing where you are weak. If the denial of a problem was the key to overcoming it, I would say, "let's lie to ourselves and become the champions we all long to be." In reality, if we lie about it, we'd be no more useful than a fake movie set. We'd have the appearance of strength on the outside, but there would be no truth to our strength on the inside where it counts most. One strong push of temptation on the outside and it will all fall in. Remember, "what is" isn't necessarily "what will always be," but it is what it is and it needs to be recognized for what it is.

Joseph was no dummy; he could look around at everyone else and see that in comparison he was not hard to look at. When someone has been given the benefit of great looks or any attribute the opposite sex finds attractive, it will be noticeable even to the one who has it. The "it" that Joseph had

> A wise man understands temptation often travels down the same road blessing traverses.

was twofold; first, he was physically handsome in form and appearance. Second, he had the favor of God on his life and was climbing the corporate structure. There is absolutely nothing wrong with being attractive and blessed by God within your career; in fact, it is truly a blessing if you have both. There is nothing wrong with it at all, but a wise man understands temptation often travels down the same road blessing traverses.

Joseph couldn't have missed the fact Potiphar's wife was looking at him, not like a mother, but like an admiring lover. I am sure as he walked by, he could see her admiring gaze out of the corner of his eye. It's not hard to spot lustful eyes, especially if they are aimed your way. Joseph recognized this presented an opportunity: an opportunity to fail or succeed. When we look at temptation, we must remember these tests are never to see if we will stay the same, but to see if we will move forward or move back. The same attack which the enemy leverages to move you backward will also bring with it an opportunity to grow into the person you are destined to become.

Ways to recognize your areas of temptation:

- **Your history.** It's clearly something you struggle with. Sometimes you just know that this is something you have always struggled with and anytime you are faced with it, it's going to be a struggle.
- **Your surroundings**. Is there anything in your current environment, be it work, church, or even where you live, that presents something that could lead to a trap? Many times you will see something presently occurring in your environment and just the fact that you are taking time to recognize it will give you the ability to avoid any trap set by the enemy.
- **Someone you trust points it out.** There are many leaders who could have avoided destruction if they simply would have recognized the danger that was being pointed out by their spouse or best friend.

Joseph did not have anyone warning him of the dangers awaiting him at Potiphar's house, but he did recognize the potential for derailment at the hands of his master's wife.

Nothing is as important as just being honest with yourself and being open to seeing things as they really are. It's as simple as realizing your excitement for an upcoming trip is because there will be no one to watch everything you do. It does not matter what vice waits for you, if you will be honest enough to recognize it for what it really is, and talk about it with someone you trust, temptation will have less power in the light than it does in the darkness. Recognizing it won't guarantee you will not fall prey to it, but it gives you a much better chance if you do.

Why do we want to keep our eyes wide open and recognize temptation before we fall into it?

> Lest Satan should take advantage of us; for
> we are not ignorant of his devices. 2 Cor. 2:11

Resistance. Look up the definition of the word resistance in almost any dictionary and you will find a recurring use of one word: oppose. In simplest terms, it means to fight against something. A word picture that describes this is an army turning right into the enemy to stop them from advancing into their territory. It is the picture of an army resisting the attack and the advance of the enemy. As Christians, we've been given the call to resist the attacks of the enemy—and the power to do so.

Joseph was aware of the trap being set for him by Potiphar's wife; she not only pursued him, but she strategically waited until no one was in the house. So, he dug in his heels and steeled himself to resist.

- Resist in his own heart. He formed a thought and made a heart decision.
- Resist in his words. He declared that decision out loud.
- Resist in his will. He acted on his heart and he acted on his words.

When it comes to resistance, sometimes you have to turn around and go another direction. Sometimes you have to do more than just turn around; sometimes you need to run like Joseph did. I know someone who moved his family to another area because the environment he was in was set up to cause failure for him. What are you willing to do to resist the plans of the enemy?

The Bible has a lot to say about resistance:

> Therefore submit to God. Resist the devil and he will flee from you. James 4:7

> Put on the whole armor of God, that you may be able to stand against the wiles of the devil. Eph. 6:11

> You have not yet resisted to bloodshed, striving against sin. Heb. 12:4

There is no doubt: when it comes to temptation, we all must resist. Whether it's resisting our own weakness, or resisting the plan of the enemy to trap us, either way we need to learn how to strongly resist.

Joseph's relationship with God was the source of his strength for resisting temptation—not his own strength or will-power. Even when we fail to resist, it is never a failure of God's power in us, but rather our human weakness that keeps us from being fully perfect. Thank God for His grace and mercy.

Reasoning. In the encounter Joseph had with the wife of Potiphar, he also used the power of reasoning in his response.

> She said, "Lie with me." But he refused and said to his master's wife, "Look, my master does not know what is with me in the house, and he has committed all that he has to my hand. There is no one greater in this house than I, nor has he kept back anything from me but you, because you are his wife. How then can I do this great wickedness, and sin against God?" So it was, as she spoke to Joseph day by day, that he did not heed her, to lie with her or to be with her. Gen. 39:7-10

In this scripture, Joseph makes a clear case why he will not give in to her advances. He begins with his own position, recognizing he has been given a trust that is not to be violated. Joseph understands the responsibility he has been given and he uses that as a defense against her advances—a great point to consider when one is responding to temptation. When faced with temptation, consider what you have to lose versus what you hope to gain.

Joseph is crystal-clear: it would be wrong to betray his master, but more than that it would be a history-changing biblical blunder to betray the God who gave him this position.

There are three things we should always consider before we respond to temptation—questions we can ask ourselves.

1. How will this decision affect me and my current position in life? Sometimes just the realization there will be consequences for our decisions can give us all the reasoning power

> **When faced with temptation, consider what you have to lose versus what you hope to gain.**

we need to choose the proper response to temptation. On more than one occasion when I was a state trooper, I had someone offer me cash to let them go instead of arresting them for possession of illegal drugs. While I was almost nearly broke during my tenure as a trooper, and a thousand dollars in cash would have helped a lot, I was already fully aware of the consequences I would face once I was caught.

I can hear you now: "But no one would have ever found out! If he confessed to paying you off, he would have gone to jail as well." The thing I knew through good, old-fashioned common sense reasoning was even if I let him go, he would have eventually been arrested for something else. When he did, the first thing he would've said to the officer or state attorney would be something like, "If you guys give me a break, I will tell you about a crooked cop who took cash from me in exchange for letting me go free." You see, that reasonable reality had the power to help me always respond correctly no matter what someone offered me. I had reasoned it out: the only thing I was being offered was a chance to end my career early and go to jail.

2. How will this decision affect others? It's easy to see Joseph knew this would have a negative impact not only on his master, but also his master's marriage. So many affairs could be stopped before they ever started if the tempted parties took enough time to reasonably think about all the individuals who would be hurt—if not destroyed. Our sins always hurt someone else—sometimes people we know and sometimes people we may never meet. In my time as an adult, I have seen several leaders who made wrong and even illegal decisions. Some of these decisions were even far-reaching enough to cause people to lose jobs and incomes. If you grew up in my generation or were alive during the sixties and early seventies, the name Richard Nixon will forever be linked with the word Watergate. I am sure he'd do a lot of things differently now if he had the chance.

I have the incredible honor of being a grandfather to four granddaughters. It provides so many joys and thrills; being a grandparent is one of the most wonderful surprises in life—I simply love it!

Another wonderful thing that comes with these sweet little granddaughters is I am now creating the legacy that will not only be the brushstrokes of their childhood memories, but will color the stories retold to their kids and grandkids as well. That picture helps me move away from any situation I perceive as a "legacy destroyer." Yes, God can forgive, and your grandkids will always love you if you truly change, but why make it their job to recover what you have lost? Think about the future; think about the people you will impact if you jump down that rabbit hole of temptation.

3. How will this decision affect God and His Kingdom? There was nothing as strong as the statement Joseph uttered: "How then could I do such a wicked thing and sin against God?"

When Joseph thought about all the consequences, the strongest one is found in this statement. How could he sin against God?

We go through life afraid of what we might lose, or who we might disappoint or hurt, but how many times do we think about the effect our responses might have upon God? Our sin won't topple His kingdom or destroy His plans, but if we love God there should be a resistance to hurting or disappointing Him. Most theologians call this "the fear of the Lord."

The best way I know how to explain this is by my own upbringing as a child. My parents are some of the best parents on all the earth and I am truly blessed to be born to them. My dad and mom didn't just encourage me in life; they showed up and cheered me on. Didn't matter if it was Friday night football under the small-town lights or starting a church of my own; they always encouraged me. I really love my parents and the thought of hurting them or disappointing them has kept me from making a lot of bad decisions. Mind you, I was never perfect—none of us are—but I can recall a few times when the thought of how something would affect my parents kept me from making a bad decision.

This same principle holds true of a God who loves us unconditionally; that love should have power over the decisions we make. "Fear of the Lord" is not being afraid of God. Fear of the Lord is loving God so much you never want to hurt or disappoint Him. That is why Scripture states, "The fear of the Lord is the beginning of wisdom, and the knowledge of the Holy One is understanding" (Prov. 9:10).

When we draw near to God and come to know and love Him, we find not only a reason for living, but also the power to overcome sin and temptation.

Removal. There are times when the only response you should have to temptation is to remove the item, the person, or yourself from the environment.

The Bible tells us in Matthew 18:9: "And if your eye causes you to sin, pluck it out and cast it from you. It is better for you to enter into life with one eye, rather than having two eyes, to be cast into hell fire."

Those sound like hard words, but it is God's way of saying, "If you are struggling with alcohol, quit bartending." Or "if you are struggling with pornography, get rid of the cable and the computer." Removing yourself, the items, or the people may not guarantee you will never fall; it just makes it a lot harder to do so.

One tip I'll give you is this: when you make the decision to remove yourself or the item of temptation, make it as difficult to reverse as possible. Sometimes that can be accomplished just by telling someone else about your pitfall as well.

I know someone who was tired of eating potato chips, so they made the decision to throw the entire unopened bag in the trash so they'd be forced to stop. Well, I hate to admit it, but I was that person—and I actually went back to dig through the trash to see if I could find them. I would have done better to have opened the bag and poured the chips out into that nasty trash. Then it would have been too gross to go back into the garbage for the savory snack that was keeping me ensnared.

When you find yourself struggling, take time to:

Recognize it. Get a good grasp of what you actually struggle with. Be honest with yourself.

Resist it. Begin in your heart; make the decision you are going to resist and fight against it. Draw near to God; He's where the real power of resistance comes from.

Reason. Take time to consider the cost. List all the reasons why it's not worth it.

Remove it. If you can't overcome it with the first three tools, then remove the item, the person, or yourself. Don't forget to tell someone you trust as an added layer of security.

"Then the chief butler told his dream to Joseph, and said to him, 'Behold, in my dream a vine was before me, and in the vine were three branches; it was as though it budded, its blossoms shot forth, and its clusters brought forth ripe grapes. Then Pharaoh's cup was in my hand; and I took the grapes and pressed them into Pharaoh's cup, and placed the cup in Pharaoh's hand.'

And Joseph said to him, 'This is the interpretation of it: The three branches are three days. Now within three days Pharaoh will lift up your head and restore you to your place, and you will put Pharaoh's cup in his hand according to the former manner, when you were his butler. But remember me when it is well with you, and please show kindness to me; make mention of me to Pharaoh, and get me out of this house. For indeed I was stolen away from the land of the Hebrews; and also I have done nothing here that they should put me into the dungeon.'

Now it came to pass on the third day, which was Pharaoh's birthday, that he made a feast for all his servants; and he lifted up the head of the chief butler and of the chief baker among his servants. Then he restored the chief butler to his butlership again, and he placed the cup in Pharaoh's hand…Yet the chief butler did not remember Joseph, but forgot him."

Gen. 40:9-15, 20-23

CHAPTER 7

RESPONDING TO THE WAIT

I don't know anyone who likes to wait.

As infants, we cry to be fed instead of waiting for food to come. As adults, we may not cry like we did as babies, but the feeling is the same: we hate to wait. We may acknowledge there are things *worth* waiting for, but if we are honest, the process of waiting is not easy for anyone.

Joseph's story is a case study on waiting. He waited decades for a destiny he foresaw very early in his life. Very few things test us more on our leadership journey than waiting.

Joseph's story ends with a happy family reunion and a position of authority where he was instrumental to the survival of the entire country—and it's a great read. But remember, it didn't happen overnight. While it takes less than an hour to read the account

> While it takes less than an hour to read the account of Joseph in Genesis, it took much longer to live out.

of Joseph in Genesis, it took much longer to live out. Let's compare his story to ours in the context of time.

Where were you thirteen years ago? If you can remember that far back, imagine if your life was in a season of challenge you had never faced before. Now imagine you didn't know the end of the story—or if there would even be a happy ending.

I think that's why it is so hard for us to see this for what it was: a thirteen year; 4,745 day; 113,880 hour period of waiting—and *not* waiting in a place of comfort. Just think of when Joseph was in prison: after interpreting the head cupbearer's dream, the cupbearer forgot all about Joseph and never told Pharaoh as he had promised. I can almost picture Joseph packing his things in expectation of his release. Yet he remained in prison for two more years, until Pharaoh's dream jogged the memory of the cupbearer. Let's keep it in perspective: there is a big difference between someone

> **How we respond to times of waiting will be a key determinant to what happens in our life.**

waiting to get a promotion and someone waiting to get out of jail. That's exactly why this amazing story is full of truth we can apply when we find ourselves in the most difficult times of waiting. How we respond to times of waiting will be a key determinant to what happens in our life.

Joseph was not the only person in Scripture who had to wait; almost every major figure in both the New and Old Testament experienced a period of waiting. Joseph, however, set a powerful and specific pattern of how we should respond to life's waiting rooms—patterns which can help us move forward.

Joseph didn't give up. While we can't read everything that Joseph thought, it is clear he found something to hang on to, something to keep living for. Belief is a very powerful thing; in this life, belief can be the difference between continuing on or giving up.

Within every story you read of soldiers who survived torture as POW's, you always find an element of belief; something that kept them believing they would eventually be released. Without belief, it would have been easier to succumb to death than to continue to suffer the horrible circumstances of imprisonment.

I love the true story of Colonel Sanders.[3] When he was just six years old, his father died and his mother was forced to obtain employment. He became responsible for watching after and cooking for his siblings. It's been told that by seven he was a pretty good cook. After that, his life was full of all kinds of jobs, until he eventually entered the gasoline business as a service station owner in Corbin, Kentucky—where he first began serving food to customers, specializing in southern dishes. Word spread quickly about the great food there, and he shut the gas pumps down to turn it into a restaurant.

Now if you didn't know the full story of his life you might guess his one restaurant grew into what we know as Kentucky Fried Chicken. While it's true these early successes were part of the journey that took the Colonel to the top of the chicken world, you would be remiss to think it was that easy. Through a series of events, he actually sold that location and, at the age of sixty-five, he and his wife found themselves driving around the nation with his signature pressure cookers and the dream of seeing his famous chicken become a franchise. There are some who say he even slept in his car as he went from restaurant to restaurant, trying to get them to sell his famous chicken.

The dream finally took off when he began to find restaurants that would partner with him. His big break came when John Y. Brown, Jr. and Jack C. Massey offered to buy the franchise rights. In 1965, Sanders sold the rights to the franchise for $2 million dollars. What was the secret to Colonel Sanders' success? His blend of secret spices? No! He just never gave up. He responded to the hardship and obstacles by never giving up. Did he have to wait decades before he became successful? Was the wait worth it? Take a lesson from Joseph and from Colonel Sanders: if you want what you are waiting for, quitting is not an option.

He didn't compromise. One of the pitfalls in being patient is the temptation to compromise. I have seen this firsthand in my own life. I start with one thing in mind, but the longer I have to wait the more I become willing to change my mind and settle for less—simply because I can have second-best now, and that seems easier than continuing to endure patiently.

Think of Joseph and how long he waited, even after he was forgotten in prison. How many of us would have been open to a better deal, or any offer to be released from our prison of waiting? Not Joseph, and the reason I know this is based on his response when he was brought before Pharaoh to interpret Pharaoh's dream.

In Genesis 41:14-16 it says:

> Then Pharaoh sent and called Joseph, and they brought him quickly out of the dungeon; and he shaved, changed his clothing, and came to Pharaoh. And Pharaoh said to Joseph, "I have had a dream, and there is no one who can interpret it. But I have heard it said of you that you can understand a dream, to interpret

it." So Joseph answered Pharaoh, saying, "It is
not in me; God will give Pharaoh an answer
of peace."

Joseph acted as he had always acted, giving credit for his ability to God. The ability to interpret dreams had not handed Joseph the "get out of jail free" card he had hoped after interpreting the head cupbearer's dream. Instead he was forgotten and remained in prison. He could have become discouraged, given up the gift when it did not immediately supply his freedom. He could have compromised his own convictions, but Joseph's faith in God remained steadfast.

Winston Churchill is famous for being a man of convictions who had to wait through a world war for victory. Like Joseph, he never compromised—although opportunities for compromise were available much earlier in the process. An excerpt from his famous 1941 speech at his alma mater, Harrow School, exemplifies his resolution to stick with his convictions despite the months of being attacked by air and threatened with invasion:

Surely from this period of ten months this is the
lesson: never give in, never give in, never, never,
never, never—in nothing, great or small, large
or petty—never give in except to convictions
of honor and good sense. Never yield to force;
never yield to the apparently overwhelming
might of the enemy. We stood all alone a year
ago, and to many countries it seemed that

our account was closed, we were finished. All this tradition of ours, our songs, our school history, this part of the history of this country, were gone and finished and liquidated.[4]

He allowed his faith to be deepened. As we see in Joseph's encounter with Pharaoh, he did not shrink or become weak in faith during his thirteen years of waiting. Joseph's faith grew and increased in strength. The long years of suffering, forgotten in prison, could have broken him down and pushed him backwards. Instead, it had the opposite effect, deepening his faith and causing him to grow. Real growth always happens in the waiting room of life if we have the right attitude.

> **Real growth always happens in the waiting room of life if we have the right attitude.**

What is it about waiting that causes us to grow in faith and become stronger? Think of Abraham Lincoln; his journey to the White House was one obstacle after another. Would he have ever guessed that his resume would look like this?

In 1832 he lost his job.
In 1832 he was defeated in an election for legislature.
In 1833 he failed in business.
In 1834 he was elected to legislature.
In 1835 his sweetheart died.
In 1836 he had a nervous breakdown.
In 1838 he was defeated in a vote for Speaker.

112

In 1839 he was defeated for nomination to Congress.

In 1846 he was elected to Congress.

In 1848 he lost re-nomination.

In 1849 he was rejected as land officer.

In 1854 he was defeated in election for Senate.

In 1856 he was defeated in nomination for Vice President.

In 1858 he was defeated in election for Senate.

In 1860 he was elected as President of the United States.

Now that is long list of losses and waiting, but as you read some of Lincoln's writings, you will find he was being strengthened. He was being prepared for a position of leadership that would take great confidence. Like Joseph, he responded to the waiting by growing—growing in faith.

No matter where you are stalled out, your current place of waiting is the best place to grow and prepare for your future landing spot, where you will need the strength and faith you acquired in your time of growing.

I love what the Apostle James writes, especially in The Message translation of the Bible:

> Consider it a sheer gift, friends, when tests and challenges come at you from all sides. You know that under pressure, your faith-life is forced into the open and shows its true colors. So don't try to get out of anything prematurely. Let it do its work so you become mature and well-developed, not deficient in any way. James 1:4-8 (MSG)

He rested in God. What does it mean to rest in God? It simply means you are trusting God and have taken your hands off the steering wheel. You're allowing God to do His work; to act as the GPS to your destination. This is what I like to call "active surrender." You are fulfilling your daily duties and going to work, but inside you have given this to God; it's in His hands.

It is apparent Joseph reached that place of resting in God. The encounter with Pharaoh is like a DNA test, revealing Joseph's character and thoughts. I have no doubt Joseph peacefully surrendered to waiting on God. Ultimately we are all waiting on God

Resting in God is waiting on God.

when it comes to the important issues of life. We are not waiting for Mr. Smith to give us a job or Ms. Right to come around the corner and introduce herself to us; no, we are waiting on God. Resting in God is waiting on God.

When someone is not waiting on God, but instead waiting for circumstances or people to funnel them to their destiny, they become filled with both anxiety and fear.

How can you find peace and rest in difficult times? By making a clear decision about who you believe has the power to open the right door or close the wrong one. In essence, you must rest your faith on God to be the one who opens the door.

Isaiah 26:3 reminds us of God's response when we choose to rest in Him, fully focusing on and steadfastly trusting in Him: "You will keep him in perfect peace, whose mind is stayed on you, because he trusts in You."

There came a point on my journey from Texas back to Florida that I had to rest in God. I found I could have peace despite the crisis around me. When we have entered the rest of the Lord, we not only find peace but more importantly we find that God works on our behalf while we wait. The truth is, if you're not resting in God then you're really not waiting on God.

Why do we have to wait? It seems like a fair question to ask, doesn't it? We ask this question all the time, whether waiting in line for a coffee at Starbucks or waiting for your spouse to get ready. Usually what we mean is, "Why is this taking so long?" No matter how we look at it, no one ever signs up for extra waiting hours at the doctor's office. No one refuses a

> The truth is, if you're not resting in God then you're really not waiting on God.

"fast pass" to get to the front of the line quicker. So is there a reason God would make us wait for something in life? And what would that reason be? There are two reasons.

You are not ready. All you have to do is look through scripture to see many examples of people who were not ready for what God had called them to do. He made them wait until they were ready. Everyone from the Apostle Paul, to Moses, even young Jesus had to go through a period of time called preparation.

God has sent many into the school of waiting simply to prepare them for where He is sending them. This school of delay is not punishment, but preparation. Some of the greatest business minds and world leaders of our day have been through this school, and there was not one wasted minute of preparation time. They are proof that more is achieved in the process than in getting the position itself.

Think of Joseph and all he needed to learn before he could lead Egypt. He needed to understand the customs and manners of those in leadership, and most of all he needed to learn the language. There was no better place to learn those things than in the house of Potiphar. What may have looked like punishment was really preparation. The question we must ask ourselves when we are parked somewhere is, "What are we supposed to learn while we are here?"

This happened to me in my journey back to Florida from Texas to plant a church. The only job I could find was at Chase Bank, in the credit card division. I was a service-to-sales advisor. My job was simple: address your question or need, then sell you one of our products. I really hated the job in the beginning and I thought often of quitting. Why did God bring me to this place? How long would I have to serve there? It wasn't until I asked God my favorite question that I got an answer:

"God, what do you want me to do?"

"Ask me to bless you at Chase."

I remember thinking, "I don't want to be blessed here, I want to *leave* here." No matter what I said or thought, those were the final instructions from God. After a few days, I finally stopped fighting God's plan and I started resting in God. I asked Him to bless me and make me a great salesperson with lots of sales. I'd love to tell you it was easy, but I would be lying to you and everyone else reading this book. It did, however, became easier each day when I prayed that same prayer as I parked my car.

A year after that prayer, I had gone from being at the bottom of the sales ladder to winning the award for the top salesperson in my entire division. I went on to win the same award again the next year. The biggest reward was this: if I had not gotten the experience I received from working there, I would never have been hired for my job in Christian publishing. I am where I am today because God made me wait at Chase for two years.

Sometimes God will make us wait because "it" is not ready. Think again of Joseph's journey: if he had been too early, many would have died. If he had been too late, the same thing would have happened. Timing is everything. I believe God doesn't mind giving us a flat tire on the way to an interview to prevent us from taking the wrong job. We've all heard stories of people who couldn't find the person they were supposed to marry until later in life, but in the end they were worth the wait.

Right now you may feel like you're being passed over for something; like you're stuck. What if you knew God was delaying you to give you something so much better? Are you wrestling or resting?

You have a choice. You can attempt to force God's hand, pushing for what you want, or you can allow Him to support you in the place and position you are in, relaxing in Him. The first will exhaust you; the second will refresh you and enable you to grow. Nothing shows you trust God more than waiting. Just ask Abraham.

Let's take a look at the story of King Saul, a man who was unwilling to wait and chose his own way.

> When the men of Israel saw that they were in danger (for the people were distressed), then the people hid in caves, in thickets, in rocks, in holes, and in pits. And some of the Hebrews crossed over the Jordan to the land of Gad and Gilead.
>
> As for Saul, he was still in Gilgal, and all the people followed him, trembling. Then he waited seven days, according to the time set by Samuel. But Samuel did not come to Gilgal; and the people were scattered from him. So Saul said, "Bring a burnt offering and peace offerings here to me." And he offered the burnt offering. Now it happened, as soon as he had finished presenting the burnt offering, that Samuel came; and Saul went out to meet him, that he might greet him.
>
> And Samuel said, "What have you done?"
>
> Saul said, "When I saw that the people were scattered from me, and that you did not come within the days appointed, and that the Philistines gathered together at Michmash, then I said, 'The Philistines will now come down

on me at Gilgal, and I have not made suppli-
cation to the Lord.' Therefore I felt compelled,
and offered a burnt offering."

And Samuel said to Saul, "You have done fool-
ishly. You have not kept the commandment
of the Lord your God, which He commanded
you. For now the Lord would have established
your kingdom over Israel forever. But now
your kingdom shall not continue. The Lord has
sought for Himself a man after His own heart,
and the Lord has commanded him to be com-
mander over His people, because you have
not kept what the Lord commanded you."
1 Sam. 13:6-14

How do we wait? We wait in faith, expectation, and trust,
believing if we are waiting on something that good is going
to come out of it.

The best way to wait is to run and wait at the same time.
That sounds like an oxymoron, but when you read Habakkuk
2:2-3, it is evident waiting on God requires an active faith
that is on-the-move *with* God. Yes, you may be stuck at a
call center but your faith is running, running with the vision of
God. There are people on the move who are going nowhere,
and there are people in prison taking steps toward their destiny every day. There are no wasted moments, hours, days,
weeks, or years for those who are waiting on God.

Then the Lord answered me and said: "Write the vision and make it plain on tablets, that he may run who reads it. For the vision is yet for an appointed time; but at the end it will speak, and it will not lie. Though it tarries, wait for it; because it will surely come, it will not tarry. Hab. 2:2-3

Joseph responded to waiting by waiting in faith, by resting in God. He needed the time to prepare and he needed to prepare for the right time.

What are you currently waiting for and what is currently waiting for you to be prepared?

"Then it came to pass, at the end of two full years, that Pharaoh had a dream; and behold, he stood by the river. Suddenly there came up out of the river seven cows, fine looking and fat; and they fed in the meadow. Then behold, seven other cows came up after them out of the river, ugly and gaunt, and stood by the other cows on the bank of the river.

Then Pharaoh sent and called Joseph... Pharaoh said to Joseph, 'I have had a dream, and there is no one who can interpret it. But I have heard it said of you that you can understand a dream, to interpret it.'

Then Joseph said to Pharaoh, 'The dreams of Pharaoh are one; God has shown Pharaoh what He is about to do...Indeed seven years of great plenty will come throughout all the land of Egypt; but after them seven years of famine will arise, and all the plenty will be forgotten in the land of Egypt; and the famine will deplete the land.'

Then Pharaoh said to Joseph, 'Inasmuch as God has shown you all this, there is no one as discerning and wise as you. You shall be over my house, and all my people shall be ruled according to your word; only in regard to the throne will I be greater than you.'"

Gen. 41:1-3, 14-15, 25, 29-30, 39-41

CHAPTER 8

RESPONDING TO PROMOTION

Throughout Joseph's journey, we witness his choices as he responds to one difficult situation after another. We started with this principle: God's way of choosing and developing great leaders is based on the way we respond to life's challenges and obstacles.

Some might read that and assume it means every challenge will be negative and difficult. Instead, look at every challenge as a possibility to move into the next level of purpose and position God has for you. Joseph's three greatest challenges were opportunities which propeled him to a deeper level of supervision and authority. We first see it within the house of Potiphar, after he had been sold into slavery by his own brothers:

> The Lord was with Joseph, and he was a suc-
> cessful man; and he was in the house of his
> master the Egyptian. And his master saw that
> the Lord was with him and that the Lord made
> all he did to prosper in his hand. So Joseph
> found favor in his sight, and served him. Then
> he made him overseer of his house, and all that
> he had he put under his authority. So it was,
> from the time that he had made him overseer
> of his house and all that he had, that the Lord
> blessed the Egyptian's house for Joseph's sake;
> and the blessing of the Lord was on all that he

had in the house and in the field. Thus he left all that he had in Joseph's hand, and he did not know what he had except for the bread which he ate. Now Joseph was handsome in form and appearance. Gen. 39:2-6

The next time we see Joseph promoted is within the walls of a prison; it's after he was falsely accused of attempting to take advantage of his master's wife. Potiphar, who at one time entrusted Joseph with everything he owned, had placed him in prison:

So it was, when his master heard the words which his wife spoke to him, saying, "Your servant did to me after this manner," that his anger was aroused. Then Joseph's master took him and put him into the prison, a place where the king's prisoners were confined. And he was there in the prison. But the Lord was with Joseph and showed him mercy, and He gave him favor in the sight of the keeper of the prison. And the keeper of the prison committed to Joseph's hand all the prisoners who were in the prison; whatever they did there, it was his doing. The keeper of the prison did not look into anything that was under Joseph's authority, because the Lord was with him; and whatever he did, the Lord made it prosper. Gen. 39:19-23

After finding favor with the warden, a third opportunity for promotion presented itself to Joseph. Pharaoh, the leading ruler of the land, called upon him to interpret a dream. Others had attempted to interpret the dream and were put to death when they could not. Somehow Joseph confidently trusted God to give him the answer Pharaoh was looking for, and in reward he was promoted to the highest position in Egypt outside of Pharaoh himself.

> Then Pharaoh said to Joseph, "Inasmuch as God has shown you all this, there is no one as discerning and wise as you. You shall be over my house, and all my people shall be ruled according to your word; only in regard to the throne will I be greater than you." And Pharaoh said to Joseph, "See, I have set you over all the land of Egypt." Then Pharaoh took his signet ring off his hand and put it on Joseph's hand; and he clothed him in garments of fine linen and put a gold chain around his neck. And he had him ride in the second chariot which he had; and they cried out before him, "Bow the knee!" So he set him over all the land of Egypt. Gen. 41:39-43

Overall, Joseph was promoted three times; the last promotion the greatest one of all. In all three positions, he was given authority to oversee and direct others. Why is it important to look at how Joseph responded to three favorable promotions?

Because nothing has ruined more leaders than the power and authority they found in their new perch of prominence.

Remember Enron? Those in power didn't fail because they were mistreated. Failure came as a consequence of mishandled power.

We all know at least one leader who lost it all because he did not respond well to acquiring power and authority. From politics to corporations to church leaders, there are too many stories of great leaders who got off track or became corrupt in the process of leading others.

Growing up I had a lot of heroes, especially those in the church. I still remember the moment when I heard Jimmy Swaggart admitted to a moral failure. At the time, I was trying to go to his college in Baton Rouge because I was such a loyal follower of his ministry. There were many just like me who were handed a concrete reminder that man is always fallible and subject to failure.

While the reality of that helps me not to lose all faith in leadership, I did want to find the keys to how someone could rise to a position of authority without automatically falling off the ladder of success. It was important to me, a young man with a desire to lead others spiritually one day, to discover how I could avoid those pitfalls. While it was important to forgive and pray for those who had fallen, I also wanted to avoid the road they had traveled down. In my studies, I came up with three spiritual leaders I wanted to model my life after: Joseph, Daniel, and Billy Graham.

Why does power have such undesirable consequences attached to it? What is it about a leadership role that causes some leaders to chase desires that will leave them ship-wrecked? It's almost enough to make one want to avoid any role in leadership.

Lord Acton, one of the great personalities of the nine-teenth century who made the history of liberty his life's work, famously said: "Power tends to corrupt and absolute power corrupts absolutely."

Nothing increases the opportunity to fall like climbing the ladder of success, but we should not fear failure and thus draw back from becoming a great leader. Instead, we should learn how to avoid failure and follow the call to leadership. Why? Because the world needs great, extraor-dinary leaders.

While Joseph did a lot more than just climb the corpo-rate ladder of success; he made it to the top without lying, stealing, committing adultery, taking a bribe, or arranging for someone to get a special payment or favor. Think about it: if anyone had opportunities to be detoured—or worse, led astray by power—it was Joseph. Consider how his story began: rejection, slavery, the rises and falls of his subsequent journey into servanthood, prison, and a meteoric rise to high power. If anyone was headed for a "power trip," it should have been Joseph. I have seen people with painful, abusive pasts rise into positions of power and authority, and all the pain of their experience manifests, transforming them into a dictator. Thankfully, there have also been some inspiring leaders, just like Joseph, who have overcome abusive upbringings, and responded to their challenges by making an intentional choice to pursue wholehearted leadership.

How did Joseph respond to receiving power and authority? What intentional choices did he make that kept him from misusing it?

This is key: Joseph's choices were actually made well before he was thrust into a position of power and authority. These choices were not made as a response to being *given* authority, but they nonetheless laid the very path he walked to arrive at his position of leadership. I call them "pre-decisions."

Pre-decisions are battle lines and boundaries we have drawn in our heart, which show themselves at the appropriate time. A good example of this would be when you're going to lunch with a friend, and you set your mind beforehand to order from the low-calorie menu. You pull it up online and mentally and emotionally make your choice before entering the "temptation zone." If you're like me, you may have tried to do this before you go, but end up at a different restaurant, hungry and with no pre-decision made. With no pre-decision made, I end up making a decision out of my strongest emotion....hunger! Making your decision before the moment gives you the power to make the decision in the moment.

> **Making your decision before the moment gives you the power to make the decision in the moment.**

WHAT WERE THE PRE-DECISIONS THAT JOSEPH MADE?

There were three very powerful pre-decisions Joseph made that had a profound impact on how he handled his newfound authority.

He chose God. We know this is true because the Bible tells us God was with him. Simply put, the surest path to opportunity is found by following Christ and having the presence of God. Moses knew this to be true; that's why he said he would not move forward without God's presence. He knew success was not a possibility without God being present. On the other hand, Samson lost the presence of God and was so preoccupied with Delilah that God was no longer with him—and he didn't even know it. The best defense against becoming the next fallen leader is to have a real and genuine relationship with God.

I love what Moses says in Exodus 33:15: "Then he said to Him, 'if your presence does not go with us, do not bring us up from here.'"

Moses would have rather remained with his people in a place of torment and slavery than escape to the Promised Land without God. Moses had made a pre-decision: he wasn't leaving without God.

He chose purpose over position. Joseph had made the decision to seek purpose over position. He had two dreams that revealed his future and the future of his family, but there was never an indication he was seeking position over purpose. It's obvious he did not want to be sold into slavery or forgotten in prison, but it never appears he had his eye fixed on gaining a position of authority. That's what it really comes down to: we must seek purpose over position. The problem with seeking position first is it often leads us to worship the place of power instead. It can even lead you to see the position as the key to your happiness.

He chose to serve over being served. Think of King Saul and his fall from power. Even during his time of repentance with Samuel, he says: "I have sinned; yet honor me now, please, before the elders of my people and before Israel, and return with me, that I may worship the Lord your God" (1 Sam. 15:30).

Even in the midst of repentance, he wanted to be seen with Samuel so the people would continue to perceive him as their leader.

At the very core of this story, we find what is wrong with so many leaders today: the positions they fill have little to do with serving, and everything to do with being served. The real reason power can corrupt someone is because there already existed a void, a need, or a desire to be powerful and important. Getting a position of leadership should fill each of us with a sense of accomplishment. There is a difference between those who see the position as the end-all goal and those who discern the actual purpose of that position. During my own years of climbing the ladder in both the church and the corporate world, I found each heightened level came with an increased need for personal sacrifice and willingness to serve others. It became less and less about me, and more and more about them.

I love what Robert Greenleaf, author of the book *Servant Leadership*, states about leadership: "Good leaders must first become good servants."[5]

Joseph was a good leader because he was first a good servant. That was a decision he had already made in his heart, and it revealed itself at Potiphar's house, in the jail, and in the court of Pharaoh. It's one reason I don't believe Joseph was intent on merely seeking position: someone who is doing all they can to gain power is usually someone who has difficulty serving others. They are not a very valuable servant—and thus, many times they also fail to become an exceptional leader.

While Joseph's pre-decisions laid the foundation for his success as a leader, it was how he handled the authority given to him that really set him apart.

He chose to serve and serve well. Pre-decisions are important, but it's also important we follow through once we are moved into a new position of leadership. There are many things you can do to set yourself apart as a great leader, but few of them stand out like just doing a great job with excellence. There is a time to talk and there is a time to perform. Our world is filled with eloquent speakers who can impress with brilliant words and hope-filled promises of what they will do. Words without action is simply philosophy. While the exchange of ideas is necessary to create a vision, it does not get the job done.

Eleanor Roosevelt said it well: "One's philosophy is not best expressed in words; it is expressed in the choices one makes. In the long run, we shape our lives, and we shape ourselves. The process never ends until we die. And the choices we make are ultimately our own responsibility."

Think of some of the leaders who have impacted your own life. How many of them were hard workers? How many of them had a history of doing a good job no matter what the job was?

For everyone reading this book who wants to become a person of impact, it begins with an excellent work ethic, an ethic employed in the job you currently hold. The Bible has a lot to say about work; in fact, the story of mankind begins with God giving Adam a job to do. Genesis 2:15 says, "Then the Lord God took the man and put him in the Garden of Eden to tend and keep it."

Other scriptures about work can be found in Proverbs and Colossians:

> In all labor there is profit, But idle chatter leads only to poverty. Prov. 14:23

> The hand of the diligent will rule, But the lazy man will be put to forced labor. Prov. 12:24

> Bondservants, obey in all things your masters according to the flesh, not with eyeservice, as men-pleasers, but in sincerity of heart, fearing God. Col. 3:22

Doing a good job means doing more than just the minimum. It means giving it your best in all that you do. This is the effort God really blesses, when we give our best with all our heart. You might despise your current job, but the response that will change your position—and in turn, change you—is to willingly perform the job with unrivaled excellence and a positive attitude.

Further in the chapter we read: "And whatever you do, do it heartily, as to the Lord and not to men, knowing that from the Lord you will receive the reward of the inheritance; for you serve the Lord Christ" (Col. 3:23-24).

TURNING MY JOB INTO MY MINISTRY

Back when I was just a state trooper yearning to be a pastor, I would spend hours and hours dreaming of serving God's people and helping people find Christ and the eternal life God wants all of us to have. I remember envisioning a day when I would no longer have to put on that uniform and work all of those crazy hours. I spent years going to Bible school so I could get my credentials and find a position either at my church or at one in need of a pastor. I was determined to get out of the patrol and into the ministry.

This went on for several years: the struggle between the job I dreaded and the dream job that began to seem more and more unattainable. It started to feel like the doors to ministry were bolted shut for me. I began to get discouraged, and putting on that gun and uniform grew harder and harder.

It was at that time, several years into being a state trooper, that I asked God the question that brought the answer that led to one of my greatest breakthroughs. I asked God, "What do you want me to do? I know that you have called me into the ministry and I have done everything I know to do, what do you want me to do?"

The answer I heard was not what I wanted to hear. The Lord spoke into my spirit that He wanted me to do my job and to do it well. My ministry was now just to serve and protect the many people traveling down the Florida Turnpike. The first time God told me to do my job and write tickets was after my experience with rejection amongst my co-workers, and here He was saying it again—but this time it felt like He was telling me to lay down the dream I'd been working so hard on.

The real tests God brings to us, those ones He intends to use to bless and promote us, often arrive as a request to do something we don't want to do. The pattern is evident all through scripture, through the stories of men like Abraham and Moses. The story of Abraham and Isaac is a classic. In this famous story from Genesis, God tested Abraham's willingness to obey Him by asking him to sacrifice his promised son Isaac. For years and years, Abraham and his wife Sarah believed for a baby that God had promised. A son finally arrived, and when he was a small child, God asked Abraham to offer his son's life as a sacrifice—thankfully, it was only a test of Abraham's faithfulness. Abraham passed the test, coming only a moment away from taking his own son's life. God stopped him and provided another sacrifice. Abraham proved he really did trust Him and would obey Him *no matter what*. In return for Abraham's obedience, God spoke a blessing over Abraham: his seed would be more numerous than the stars in the heaven or the sand on the seashore. That story is a great example of how God will ask us to do something we would not choose on our own—and hidden in our obedience is the doorway into the future God has planned for us.

Like Abraham and Moses, I now had to make my own decision about what to do with the words God spoke to me. How would I respond? How would I stop seeking my dream and instead focus on working hard at the job I wanted to be free from?

It didn't happen overnight. I would love to say that I had a great attitude about it, but in the beginning it was simply just an act of my will. Sometimes it just takes an act of our will despite our feelings.

I then turned my pursuit of ministry into a pursuit of fulfilling my role as a state trooper with excellence. I determined to start each day with prayer, asking the Lord to guide my daily tasks. Day in and day out I heard, "Write tickets and do a great job." I heard this for maybe ten months (though it seemed like ten years) until one day I heard something different. God answered my prayer with, "Today you will pray with a couple on the side of the road." That was new! Up until that moment it was all about just doing the job I was hired to do.

Several hours later, I found an older couple on the side of the road with a flat tire. The little old lady was so excited to see me when I drove up behind their old Buick. She quickly told me about their flat tire and asked me if I would contact AAA for them. I said I'd be glad to, and since AAA was right down the road it shouldn't take them long to get here. It was in that moment that I heard the Lord say to me, "*You* change their tire."

There is nothing I hate more than changing a tire. I mean, I have thrown my back out several times just trying to get the tire out of the trunk! But God had spoken, so I told the lady I'd change the tire. She tried to convince me to just call AAA, but she had no idea I was under orders from a higher authority.

I noticed her husband sitting in the passenger seat with his legs out on the ground and a cane in his right hand. It was clear she was the one driving. As I changed their tire, I asked where they were headed. She said, "Shands Hospital to see a specialist about my husband's heart condition." Apparently he was in very poor health and needed a miracle.

I knew then this was the couple God directed me to pray with. As I finished changing the tire, the lady offered me twenty-five dollars for helping. I thanked her but told her it was my job to help, and that I couldn't take her money. She smiled and put the money back into her purse. I went on, "While I can't take your money, there is one thing you could do for me. Would you allow me to pray for you and your husband?" She answered, "yes," as she started to cry. I prayed one of the shortest, simplest prayers I've ever prayed but you could feel the power in every word. When I finished, she hugged and thanked me. She said, "We had a word from God that someone would pray with us along the way to Gainesville and that God would heal my husband. You were that person, thank you!"

As they drove off, I sat in my patrol car and took in what had just happened. I was still for an hour or so, with thought after thought tumbling through my brain as I came to grips with what God was doing. I heard the voice of the Lord as He spoke to my heart and said these words: "I can give you a position at a church, or I can give you the whole turnpike to pastor. What do you want?" There was no doubt my choice would be the turnpike because in all my times of ministry I hadn't experienced a moment like I'd just had. It doesn't take slaying a dragon to have a lasting impact in God's Kingdom; it just takes being where He is and doing what He wants you to do.

I went on to have an amazing career as a state trooper and God used me to minister to so many people along the way. Those stories will have to be in another book, as they are too numerous to list here. I eventually retired early to

> It doesn't take slaying a dragon to have a lasting impact in God's Kingdom; it just takes being where He is and doing what He wants you to do.

enter into full-time ministry. When it no longer mattered where I served God, He gave me the keys to the door that I had tried to open by myself many years earlier.

You may feel like you are in a dead-end job, far from the destiny you long for, and you do not yet realize this position may be your path to the next open door. How you respond to your current job is more than just a key to getting to the next career level; it is the key that unlocks the door to the purpose God has waiting for you. Joseph had every right to stop and complain about where he ended up, but he didn't.

He continued to perform every task with excellence while never taking his foot off the pedal of hope. You can plan for better and still put your best foot forward in your current position while you wait.

What have you been dealt that you would like to have a re-deal over? Is your attitude making it a place of pain or a place of possibility?

Joseph responded to his new position by acting as an entrusted steward. When you look at the life of Joseph and how he responded to each test, it is clear his attitude was that of a trusted steward. The definition of a steward is someone who manages property or financial affairs for the owner. Joseph never owned anything while he was climbing the corporate ladder, but he managed and stewarded millions of

> One of the greatest tests for potential leadership is not in what you do with your own possessions but what you do with the possessions of others.

dollars. One of the greatest tests for potential leadership is not in what you do with your own possessions but what you do with the possessions of others.

Joseph responded to his new authority by never forgetting where he came from. How many times have we heard of someone who has scaled the corporate ladder—perhaps even while maintaining high ethical standards—but completely forgotten where they came from?

When I was in law enforcement, the most successful sergeants and lieutenants always remembered what it was like to be a trooper. Even though they had the responsibility to make sure troopers were doing their jobs, they never forgot what it was like to be the lowest paid worker or the first to the scene of an accident. They had to learn how to motivate and correct others without losing all sensitivity to the people they were commanding.

The best way to keep that perspective is to make a commitment to always look at life through the eyes of the people you are leading. If you are "wearing their shoes" you will see things both from their perspective and from the perspective of your new role.

When we read the story of Joseph's brothers arriving to buy food, it is easy to conclude he had not forgotten where he came from. It is unlikely that Joseph ever thought that he never belonged with the group that sold him into slavery, that he really belonged in the palace all along. He was aware that his new role and authority had been given to him by God, given to him for a special purpose.

If you have been given a new role that gives you authority over those you used to work beside, never forget you were right where they were only a few months or years ago. Give honor to God for promoting you and giving you the chance to serve those whom you now lead.

Looking for an example of someone handling authority over others with humility? Look no further than Jesus. The King of Kings brought himself down to be a servant to many.

Don't forget: remembering where you came from doesn't mean you need to stay there. It just means you embrace the opportunity to treat those underneath you like you would have wanted to be treated when you were still in their position.

"When Jacob saw that there was grain in Egypt, Jacob said to his sons, 'Why do you look at one another?' And he said, 'Indeed I have heard that there is grain in Egypt; go down to that place and buy for us there, that we may live and not die.'

Now Joseph was governor over the land; and it was he who sold to all the people of the land. And Joseph's brothers came and bowed down before him with their faces to the earth.

Then Joseph said to his brothers, 'I am Joseph; does my father still live?' But his brothers could not answer him, for they were dismayed in his presence. And Joseph said to his brothers, 'Please come near to me.' So they came near. Then he said: 'I am Joseph your brother, whom you sold into Egypt. But now, do not therefore be grieved or angry with yourselves because you sold me here; for God sent me before you to preserve life...So now it was not you who sent me here, but God; and He has made me a father to Pharaoh, and lord of all his house, and a ruler throughout all the land of Egypt.'"

Gen. 42:1-2, 6, 45:3-8

CHAPTER 9

RESPONDING TO OFFENSE

Of all the things Joseph had to respond to, nothing may have been harder than being offended.

When we think of someone who is offended, we focus on the idea that they are holding a grudge or bitterness toward someone. To offend someone is to do something that causes him or her displeasure; it also refers to when someone hurts or violates another person.

People get offended every day. The real question is how do they respond to being offended or hurt? Joseph was offended by the actions of his brothers and various others who betrayed him on his unfortunate journey. It really is a miracle Joseph never let the actions of others drive him into a lifetime of resentment and bitterness. We've all seen people who let the pain of the past turn their existence into a lifetime of bitterness. What did Joseph do to avoid the trap of Satan? How did he respond to being hurt?

In Genesis 45, when Joseph finally reveals to his brothers who he really is, he lets them off the hook for how they treated him and put all the responsibility on God. How many people do you think would have given such grace to the very ones who deserted them?

Obviously, Joseph had something inside of him a lot of other people just do not have—and it came from years of honing his ability to respond up.

Has anyone hurt you in a way that's hard to forgive? The good news is the same God who helped Joseph overcome the hurt of what his brothers (and others) did to him can also help us.

Throughout my life I've met people who are living with a bitter heart. In almost every case, I've found they are stuck; unable to move forward. Yes, they may move on and advance in life but they are never really free. Like a prisoner with a ball and chain, they move forward but are always dragged back. It may not be apparent on the outside, but on the inside they are captive in a self-made prison.

In one of the most famous parables in scripture, Jesus tells the story of a servant who was indebted to his master for more money than he could ever hope to pay back. Though the master could have treated him badly, he forgave the servant and released him from his debt. You might think the servant would be so happy to be free that nothing could offend him. Instead, the servant does the complete opposite. We quickly discover what happens to those who refuse to forgive after being forgiven: they are "delivered to the torturers until the debt is repaid."

What does that mean? They are trapped in a self-imposed prison until they turn to God, repent, and release the person they were holding the offense toward.

> Therefore the kingdom of heaven is like a certain king who wanted to settle accounts with his servants. And when he had begun to settle accounts, one was brought to him who owed him ten thousand talents. But as he was not able to pay, his master commanded that he

be sold, with his wife and children and all that he had, and that payment be made. The servant therefore fell down before him, saying, "Master, have patience with me, and I will pay you all." Then the master of that servant was moved with compassion, released him, and forgave him the debt.

But that servant went out and found one of his fellow servants who owed him a hundred denarii; and he laid hands on him and took him by the throat, saying, "Pay me what you owe!" So his fellow servant fell down at his feet and begged him, saying, "Have patience with me, and I will pay you all." And he would not, but went and threw him into prison till he should pay the debt. So when his fellow servants saw what had been done, they were very grieved, and came and told their master all that had been done. Then his master, after he had called him, said to him, "You wicked servant! I forgave you all that debt because you begged me. Should you not also have had compassion on your fellow servant, just as I had pity on you?" And his master was angry, and delivered him to the torturers until he should pay all that was due to him. So My heavenly Father also will do to you if each of you, from his heart, does not forgive his brother his trespasses. Matt. 18:23-35

I will never forget an encounter I had with a young man battling depression. He had struggled with it for years and prayed God would help him. While not every emotional struggle is also spiritual, many people who battle emotional wellbeing are also fighting spiritual forces we cannot see with our natural eyes. As a pastor, I have dealt with people whose depression was a physical problem, those with a psychological issue, and those with a spiritual ailment. While there are differences, I have found almost everyone I prayed with who dealt with depression on a spiritual or emotional level either had no relationship with God, or if they did, they had a deep-seated hurt keeping them in an emotional prison.

As I spent time with this young man, he described a mild depression that made it hard for him to truly experience joy. He never had suicidal thoughts or a desire to hurt himself; he just couldn't really experience joy. He explained he believed in Christ and had asked Him to be his savior years earlier. He loved God and loved being with other Christians. Everyone said he was very committed to the Lord.

We met once a week and prayed together for a breakthrough in his life. One day when we were praying, I asked him, "Have you ever been hurt or offended by anyone?" He thought for a moment and just shook his head "no." I explained that many times when someone is withholding forgiveness, they struggle with the same feelings he was having. He still couldn't think of anything and I didn't want to force the issue.

It was then, right before we moved on, that I felt led to ask him, "If you could ask God anything what would you ask

Him?" I saw his face change as he said, "If I could ask Him anything, I'd want to know why did He take my mother? Why did my mother have to die when I was born?"

Now I knew why I felt directed to ask that question. I knew we were on the cusp of a breakthrough.

Most people answer a question like "why did God allow that to happen?" with explanations of why God was doing something good, or why that person shouldn't feel hurt by God. I have learned not to try to explain why God allows something to happen. I have learned to just listen and be there. No one can answer those questions like God Himself, and He usually does not need my help to do that. I'm not saying God won't use a person as part of the process—He usually does—but it's in His time and not ours. We humans tend to want to fix those things immediately. We feel if we can give our explanation to the person who is hurt, they will see the light and forgive or release God from the pain they are feeling. That's right, I said forgive God! There are many people who have offenses toward God Himself. They hold Him responsible for not intervening or preventing something that brought deep pain or loss into their life.

In answer to my question, my young friend asked me again and again with tear-filled eyes, "Why did God have to take my mother? Why was I not allowed to have a mother like everyone else?" His questions exposed the truth: his mother had passed away just after he had been born, and he was harboring the pain. I looked at him and said, "I don't know why God allowed your mother to die, I really do not know, but I know that we can go to God and ask Him why.

I believe we can ask Him and somehow, at some time, He will answer if you listen."

I explained that I fully believed God answers prayers and that He would answer his somehow: through a verse of scripture, through another person, or just a "knowing" inside his spirit. With that explanation, we started to pray.

We had prayed for about thirty minutes when the young man started to cry and almost laugh a little. He looked up at me and said something no counselor or pastor could have told him with the same result. He said God told him, "I did not *take* your mother, I *gave*—I gave her eternal life with me."

> **Holding an offense is like punishing yourself for the wrong that someone else has done to you.**

The young man went on to say, "He is not a taker, but a giver and God gave my mother the most wonderful thing ever."

I knew he had finally forgiven God for his mother's passing; you could see the joy on his face. We prayed a final prayer and he went on his way, never to be depressed again. I talked to him years later and he was married and starting a whole new life for himself. He was no longer a prisoner! Holding an offense is like punishing yourself for the wrong that someone else has done to you.

There were several things that Joseph did in response to being painfully discarded by his brothers and others along the way:

He chose to trust God. He chose to see God's plan in all the trouble and trust it. To Joseph, there was a blueprint bigger than the harmful actions and malicious intentions of his brothers. Yes, they meant it for harm, but God was in charge and He meant it for good.

I have seen people make the decision to get stuck knee-deep right where their last offense happened. Someone did them wrong and they can't move on until it is resolved or the person pays for what they did. I am aware there are truly serious offenses that happen to innocent people and it is difficult to understand how anyone could see God at work in the middle of something so horrific. I don't know anyone who wouldn't give everything they owned to stop evil from happening in the world. We all wish bad things wouldn't happen to

> **The enemy has no weapon to destroy a man who will not be offended or live an unforgiving life.**

good people, but that will never be in this age. Unspeakable wrongs happen to the innocent, and while I believe the offender should go to prison if they deserve to, I don't believe the victim should sentence themselves to a prison of bitterness. It's not easy to respond like Joseph: it's very hard, but if you want to have the life and destiny God has for you, you have to find the same strength Joseph found and see God in the midst of what hurts. You may think He is not there, but He is.

As you read Chapter 45, you can almost hear Joseph smile as he tells his brothers that they were not to blame for what happened to him. Talk about freedom! The enemy has no weapon to destroy a man who will not be offended or live an unforgiving life.

When I was sitting in my totaled-out car on the side of the road in Texas, it would have been so easy to have become bitter and blame someone, including myself. I am glad I heard God say, "Choose your attitude wisely because you will remember it for the rest of your life." Now as I look back to that moment, I can see God was the one moving me through the struggles to prepare me for the role I have today, and for this book you are reading now. This does not mean God triggers evil simply to prepare us for a future. We live in a fallen world, and in this world we are going to have trouble, but for the child of God, we can trust He is going to work out all things for good. That means you can trust God to take the most painful things in life and eventually use them for good. Knowing there are many horrible things some of the people who are reading this may have gone through, I do not say this lightly. It's not easy but it is true, God can take the worst and use it for an incredible future.

Earlier in the book I shared the dance card illustration from the movie *Meet Me in St. Louis*, when the sisters wrote up an unfavorable dance card for another girl. The question is what will you and I do with the dance card life has given us? God wants us to dance through the card, trusting that every spin and twist and turn is leading us into the destiny He has planned for us.

When you are offended—and you will be offended or hurt at some point if you have not already been—how will you respond? Will you respond like Joseph did, by trusting God is still in charge even when you can't see it?

He submitted to God. Joseph did not give men power over his life. Even when they were in a position of authority, Joseph didn't relinquish the power over his life to a person.

Let me explain this in another way: when we allow another person to have supremacy in our life, we have handed them the power to make or break our future, our destiny.

Joseph never gave that power to Potiphar, Potiphar's wife, the Head Cupbearer, his brothers, or even Pharaoh. While this didn't indicate a lack of respect for those in positions of authority, it did mean he never allowed them to take the place of God in his life. If Joseph had responded to his pain by crumbling and allowing them to exert power over his life, the vines of hurt and bitterness would have climbed and spread until they cut off his ability to move and the dance would have ceased. If the dance had stopped for Joseph, he would have never made it to the palace—and he would not have been there to save everyone.

When you think about how we respond to being antagonized or insulted, and you realize the enemy hopes we'll become hurt and quit, you have to ask yourself, "Who will be affected? Who will never receive the leadership, love, direction, or wisdom they've been waiting for because we are no longer running the race that God intended for us to run?" God wants us to always give that power to Him and not to men. Ultimately, God is the only one you can trust and He has already paid for it so He should own it!

How should you respond when someone offends or hurts you?

Forgive quickly. One of the most powerful things you can do is make the decision to forgive as quickly as possible. While sometimes it is only an act of your will and not your heart, it still helps if you make the decision as early as possible.

Nothing is sadder than seeing someone who has held onto a grudge for many years. Too often the bitterness of heart has brought about dire consequences in their relationships, career, and health, eventually affecting nearly every area of life. A grudge can be very much like a cancer; if you wait too long to remove it, the damage can be too extensive to save the person. Ephesians 4:26 warns us:

> Be angry, and do not sin: do not let the sun go
> down on your wrath.

Just as it is not to our benefit to give our power away to other people, it is not beneficial to allow our emotions to rule us. Both choices are sin. Give all of your hurts to God daily and don't go to bed offended. Even if you can't approach the person who did it, make a decision in your heart to let go and let God as quickly as possible.

Ask God for help. Go to God and ask Him to help you deal with it the right way. Too many times we fail to go to God and instead we go to other people. When we go to other people with our offense, it grows and spreads; when we go to God with our offenses, they lose their power.

Consider this. Every time you are hurt or offended, Immanuel, the God who is with us, is right there with you waiting for you to ask Him for help. Just picture it. You have just suffered a blow straight to the center of your heart, the breath has been knocked right out of you, tears are pressing at the back of your eyes, and the creator of the universe is standing right behind you and leaning over your right shoulder, experiencing this great wound with you, ready to help. If we understood that God is present in every situation wanting to help us when we are hurt, wouldn't we go to Him instead of others?

It is vitally important that we also understand the motivation of the devil. If we could have a debriefing on our enemy the same way the Navy Seals are debriefed on an enemy in a foreign country, we would be able to unplug from the emotion and plug into the understanding of what is really going on. We would learn that the devil desperately hopes that we will allow the hurt and offense to sink deep within our heart where it will be difficult to remove. The devil and all his helpers work to keep us from seeing the truth about forgiving others so that we ultimately remove ourselves from the blessing of God. His goal is not only to bring harm to us as individuals, he is also setting us up to hurt others, who then hurt others.

I don't think that we need to major in the enemy and his plans to be aware of the way he works, but we need to be aware of how much he really wants to pull us into bitterness, hatred, and judgment. He knows what happens if we fail to forgive those who hurt us. Consider the saying, "Hurting people hurt other people." The enemy knows this and he is depending on it. When we choose to ask for God's help and healing, we overcome the strategy of the enemy.

Joseph had hours and hours to think after he was sold into slavery. It is estimated that he traveled over two hundred and fifty miles before he was sold into the house of Potiphar. We are not talking about a car trip to grandmother's house.

We are talking about a long hot walk. Most people would have become extremely bitter on that trip alone and they would no longer be dancing through the dance card of their life. How did Joseph not get bitter after he was treated so badly by his own family and at the same time he lost his freedom?

When you meet people who are bitter, you often find that they are bitter with family or loved ones. It's one thing when an enemy or stranger hurts you but it's another thing altogether when it's someone that you love and trust and are expecting to love you in return.

While we cannot see everything Joseph was thinking after he was sold into slavery, I know that he was making choices, choices to see possibility in the middle of tragedy, choices to not let hurt become bitterness, choices to go to God instead of man about the hurt he had received. How do I know that? I know that because he never became bitter. I know he was hurt and the hurt was real but there is no way he would have developed the capacity to treat his brothers with grace if he would have chosen to give the offense a place of power and traveled down the road of resentment moving the pain into poison. No, Joseph was doing something about his pain. Maybe it was on the road from home to Potiphar's house, on the two hundred and fifty mile walk. Maybe he decided to turn to God, and as he turned to God, he heard God's voice softly say, "I am with you and this will turn out for good." In our Christian walk, there is nothing more important than simply hearing God's voice. His voice can make sense out of everything. Just look at Jesus. In the worst hour of His life, you don't see Him talking to everyone else; you see Him alone in the garden talking to His father. You see Him talking and you see Him listening. When you are in your worst situation, your first response should be to respond up, respond up to God.

"Joseph is a fruitful bough, A fruitful bough by a well; His branches run over the wall. The archers have bitterly grieved him, Shot at him and hated him. But his bow remained in strength, And the arms of his hands were made strong By the hands of the Mighty God of Jacob."

Gen. 49:22-24

CHAPTER 10

THE OVERCOMING LIFE: RESPONDING VS. REACTING

In the end, Joseph's story illustrates how someone can live a more victorious life by *responding* to challenges and opportunities instead of just reacting to them. While we can learn from the life of Joseph, all learning must begin from a place of self-awareness. Put yourself in the sandals of Joseph: how would you have reacted to each of those situations? I've done the same self-evaluation. I'd like to think I would have done the same exact thing, but as I look at my own life, too many times I choose the instant reaction instead of leaning in to the learning curve and embracing it.

Too often, I've found myself:

- Moving too early to judgment without knowing all of the facts. I react in ignorance.
- Snapping at a friend or family member simply because I am tired and out of patience. I react out of the deficit of my own emotional state.
- Allowing internal fear to manifest in an outward statement of doubt or negativity. I react out of my own fear and doubt.
- Letting envious thoughts cause me to dislike someone simply because they have something I'd like to have. I react out of my own selfish desire and ambition.

The good news is we can all actively make the decision to change; to allow *ourselves* to be changed by the learning process. We can make the decision to become a "first responder" instead of just being a "first reactor."

THE DIFFERENCE IN RESPONDING VS. REACTING

The first step is learning to take the time to choose the best way to answer. Remember, a reaction is your first impulse or initial feeling. A first impulse is good if your house is on fire; it doesn't work as well when you're dealing with a relationship or your own fears. Responding gives time for God and your own reason to enter in. I want to make sure you understand this because it's critical: when you react, it's all you, but when you respond, it's you and God!

Always remember, God works on our behalf. Even though He has His own timetable, He is not slow to fulfill His word. He will take care of things in His time, but we have to give it to Him and be at peace knowing it's in His fully capable hands.

When you're struggling to respond, look to those who came before you in the Bible. Some of the best illustrations of greatness and leadership are a case study in choosing to respond instead of reacting. One example is David, after he and his men returned to Ziklag. They returned to camp to find that it was destroyed and everyone had been captured. If there was ever a time you'd expect someone to react with anger or vengeance, this would be it. The Bible states in 1 Samuel 30:1-8:

Now it happened, when David and his men came to Ziklag, on the third day, that the Amalekites had invaded the South and Ziklag, attacked Ziklag and burned it with fire, and had taken captive the women and those who were there, from small to great; they did not kill anyone, but carried them away and went their way. So David and his men came to the city, and there it was, burned with fire; and their wives, their sons, and their daughters had been taken captive. Then David and the people who were with him lifted up their voices and wept, until they had no more power to weep. And David's two wives, Ahinoam the Jezreelitess, and Abigail the widow of Nabal the Carmelite, had been taken captive. Now David was greatly distressed, for the people spoke of stoning him, because the soul of all the people was grieved, every man for his sons and his daughters. But David strengthened himself in the Lord his God. Then David said to Abiathar the priest, Ahimelech's son, "Please bring the ephod here to me." And Abiathar brought the ephod to David. So David inquired of the Lord, saying, "Shall I pursue this troop? Shall I overtake them?" And He answered him, "Pursue, for you shall surely overtake them and without fail recover all."

David could have given in to anger and grief—many of us would have—but instead he responded by going to God first. His men, however, chose to react. They wanted vengeance. When David didn't join them in their reactions, they turned their grief and anger on him! Most of David's men were outcasts before meeting him, so they were considering killing the very man whom had given them purpose. But, when the man of God came to them with an answer from the Lord, they finally got it right: they joined the ranks of the responders, fell into place, and followed Him. Again, as a believer in Christ, the difference between responding and reacting is that God is involved in the process when we respond, but not when we react.

Here are five important steps to take the next time you need to respond up:

1. Go to God first. Before you ask someone else, ask God.
2. Choose love. If you go to God first, He will help you do this.
3. Stay in control. If you go to God first, He will help you to do this.
4. Act in a way or respond to the person or situation in a way that God would. If you go to God first, He will help you to do this.
5. Trust God. If you go to God first...you guessed it.

I could tell you how to do some of these things on your own, without God's inspired input, but you will ultimately fail in the end. You might have step-by-step instructions but still not be able to pull it off. Why? As the Bible says, with man some things can be impossible, but with God all things are possible (Matt. 19:26).

You still need God to be in the decision-making mix, even with the steps you've learned and the stories you've heard in this book. No solutions are going to be the same. Sometimes God will tell you to "let it go," and other times He will say "take action."

Joseph epitomized this and in the end he was blessed for it. His only ally was the one who had the power and the plan to not only promote him, but to rescue millions in the process, including the lineage that our savior, Jesus Christ was born into.

See? God is in the people-saving business. He is the Alpha and the Omega, the beginning and the end. He knew the famine destined to fall upon the land. He knew that He needed to have one of His people in charge there because He could impart His wisdom on that person. It's not as if Joseph could have applied for the position of being the second most powerful man in the kingdom. God knew the path Joseph needed to have to develop that authority before the famine came.

Joseph needed to go through all he did; to go through the betrayal of his brothers, to be sold into slavery, to be falsely accused by Potiphar's wife, and to be thrown into the dungeons. The truth is this: Joseph had a divine appointment with a baker and a butler. One that would get the attention of Pharaoh in a way no one else could. Only by responding the right way through all the pain and injustice he suffered was he able to be in a position to help thousands of people survive the famine.

Remember, whatever it is you are going through, God has a plan for it. It may not be what you want, it may be unfair, and it may feel as if everyone else is against you, but just hold on! It all begins by choosing to become a first responder, instead of remaining a first reactor.

> It all begins by choosing to become a first responder, instead of remaining a first reactor.

Go to the throne for your answers. Follow God's counsel. As He did with Joseph, God will take you from the pit to the palace. And if you allow yourself to be used by Him, He will save many others along the way.

ACKNOWLEDGEMENTS

For over fifteen years, I dreamed of writing my first book. There are a lot of people to recognize, because in the end it takes a lot of people to write a book. I've always said that in order to have a great book, the author must *live* it. For me, it took more than one person to live this with me, and there are many to thank as part of this process.

First, I want to thank my team at Salem Author Services. No one has encouraged me on a daily basis more than all of you have. Every day that you asked me how my book was coming along kept me focused and accountable. I love you guys, and would not have made it to the finish line without your encouragement.

To my writing and design team: you truly are the best. Thank you, Eli Che Gonzalez; it was you who drew the book out of me and gave me the vision for it. You are an incredible ghostwriter, editor, and friend. Thank you, Dr. Larry Keefauver, for all the encouragement and mentoring you provided along the way—it always kept my eyes on the end result. Thank you to Elizabeth Vilella for all the work you did in designing the cover and website. You are truly amazing and I am so blessed to have you as a friend and designer. To Cory Callahan, thank you for being my friend through this and for the amazing pictures you took for my book and website. Most of all I have to thank my daughter, Brittnee Taylor Newman. You have not only been my editor, you have been my encourager, coach, marketing director, P.R. director, visionary leader and closest co-worker and friend in this long process. Well before my fiftieth birthday, you started challenging me to write this book and I am eternally thankful for you. I love you very much and that is why I am releasing this book on your birthday.

I have to thank my parents who always believed in me and taught me to love and follow Christ. I've never doubted God loves me and that's in large part to what you gave me: unconditional love and support. I am proud to be your son. To my children and grandchildren, you're one of the greatest reasons I write this book. My children Brittnee, Ashlee, Hunter; my son-in-law Lee Kasten, my daughter-in-law Brittany; and my precious granddaughters Paislee, Tenlee, Adalee and McKenna: I want to pass this book on to you and your future generations, that our family will always learn to respond up.

To my beautiful wife Tracee: none of this would be happening without you. Your love, support, encouragement, and guidance have been my rock and support in this venture. My life changed course when I found you and you have been at the center of every positive change in my life. There is not a story in this book you weren't a part of; this book was lived by you as much by me. Thank you for all you've done; if it wasn't for you there would be no book at all, because there would be no story. Most of all, thank you for the countless hours you've sat in your prayer chair and prayed for me and for our family. We have a story to tell in *Respond Up* because you prayed and believed. May our children's-children's-children know the influence you have had on us through your love for them and your devotion to God. I truly love you with all of my heart.

Finally I have to thank the one who made *Respond Up* possible; the one I learned to "respond up" to. Thank you Heavenly Father for your part in this book, which is on every single page. You really are the star. You have never left nor forsaken me, and you've taught me through your Holy Spirit to hear your voice and respond. Thank you for sending Jesus who not only made it possible to live forever but made a way to truly know you. Thank you for writing *Respond Up* through my experience of learning how to live life as a follower of your son, Christ Jesus.

WORKS CITED

1. Bowie, Deborah, "Everything Rises and Falls on Leadership," *Business in Greater Gainesville*, August 2015, http://business-magazinegainesville.com/everything-rises-falls-leadership

2. Godwin, Rick. Twitter, accessed November 1, 2016. https://twitter.com/ricklgodwin/status/793565648785776640

3. Felonie, Richard, "KFC founder Colonel Sanders didn't achieve his remarkable rise to success until his 60s," *Business Insider*, June 25, 2015, http://www.businessinsider.com/how-kfc-founder-colonel-sanders-achieved-success-in-his-60s-2015-6

4. "Churchill's Real "Never Give Up" Speech," *Preaching Today*, accessed October 1, 2016, http://www.preaching-today.com/illustrations/2003/january/14163.html?start=1

5. Robert K. Greenleaf. AZQuotes.com, Wind and Fly LTD, accessed November 25, 2015. http://www.azquotes.com/author/19554-Robert_K_Greenleaf,